Lida Citroën is able to help you merge the perception of who you are to yourself with who you are to the world in a completely authentic and genuine way. She has shown me, and many of our CEOs, how to take control of our reputation. Through this book, she shares the strategies and tactics needed to make it happen for anyone. This will be added to the must-read list for all our investees and clients. This is needed, relevant and usable information in today's world.
**Kevin Custer, Founding Partner, Arc Capital Development**

*Control the Narrative* is the summation of Lida Citroën's extensive work in reputation management and personal branding, working across many countries and for many years. This is a must-read for anyone looking to increase their visibility, value and impact.
**Debra Fine, keynote speaker, trainer and bestselling author**

One of the most valuable skill sets for a successful executive is their ability to control the narrative both internally and externally. *Control the Narrative* is Lida Citroën's best book yet! She has an uncanny ability for teaching executives how to build a strategy around reputation that will produce successful outcomes.
**Myron Pincomb (CAS), CEO, International Board of Credentialing and Continuing Education Standards**

A strong personal brand is essential if you want to stand out and get noticed in today's business marketplace. In *Control the Narrative*, Lida Citroën shows you exactly what it takes to discover, design and deploy an effective brand and reputation management strategy. If you want others to recognize your talents and unique contributions, read this book.
**Dorie Clark, author of *Reinventing You* and executive education faculty, Duke University Fuqua School of Business**

If you are tempted to think that personal branding is about having a nice website, a polished résumé and lots of followers on social media, stop and read this book. Personal branding is deeply rooted in your own values. Lida Citroën takes you on an amazing journey of discovering them and using them as a foundation for your unique personal brand, which will stay with you. A great read that will change the way you are seen by others and by yourself.

Jacek Ławrecki, International Communications Executive

When I need advice about personal branding, I call Lida Citroën. In *Control the Narrative*, she deftly shares her expertise in a way that we can all access. Lida shares real-world examples from leaders she has coached, which brings the book to life. She also sets out clear actions we can all take to invest in our personal brands. This is a must-read for any professional looking to leverage their career.

Morag Barrett, CEO, SkyeTeam, and author of *Cultivate: The Power of Winning Relationships* and *The Future-Proof Workplace*

As a millennial, LinkedIn is second nature to me, but Lida Citroën explained to me how to control the optics of social media to land my first sales position. Later, and through the hard work of personal brand strategy (with Lida), I secured an opportunity to lead and establish a market-disrupting sales team. If you are on the front line of your career, like me, harnessing your personal brand is effort you need to invest immediately by reading *Control the Narrative*!

Whitney Hake, Senior Vice President, Transwestern

Lida Citroën's stellar analysis of all the factors needed to compete in a post-COVID-19 world is an essential read for anyone looking to leverage their talents and get ahead. Individuals can no longer bank on a decent education and a strong résumé; they must be deliberate and intentional when thinking about their narrative. If they are not, then they could be left behind.

Jamie McLaughlin, Founder and CEO, Monday Talent

# Control the Narrative

*The executive's guide to building, pivoting and repairing your reputation*

Lida Citroën

KoganPage

**Publisher's note**

Every possible effort has been made to ensure that the information contained in this book is accurate at the time of going to press, and the publishers and authors cannot accept responsibility for any errors or omissions, however caused. No responsibility for loss or damage occasioned to any person acting, or refraining from action, as a result of the material in this publication can be accepted by the editor, the publisher or the author.

First published in Great Britain and the United States in 2021 by Kogan Page Limited

2nd Floor, 45 Gee Street
London
EC1V 3RS
United Kingdom
www.koganpage.com

122 W 27th St, 10th Floor
New York, NY 10001
USA

4737/23 Ansari Road
Daryaganj
New Delhi 110002
India

Kogan Page books are printed on paper from sustainable forests.

**ISBNs**
Hardback    978 1 3986 0084 3
Paperback   978 1 3986 0083 6
Ebook       978 1 3986 0086 7

**British Library Cataloguing-in-Publication Data**

A CIP record for this book is available from the British Library.

**Library of Congress Cataloging-in-Publication Data**

Names: Citroën, Lida, author.
Title: Control the narrative: the executive's guide to building, pivoting
    and repairing your reputation / Lida Citroën.
Description: London, United Kingdom; New York, NY: Kogan Page Limited,
    2021. | Includes bibliographical references and index.
Identifiers: LCCN 2021001358 (print) | LCCN 2021001359 (ebook) | ISBN
    9781398600843 (hardback) | ISBN 9781398600836 (paperback) | ISBN
    9781398600867 (ebook)
Subjects: LCSH: Branding (Marketing) | Reputation. | Public relations.
Classification: LCC HF5415.1255 .C4848 2021 (print) | LCC HF5415.1255
    (ebook) | DDC 658.4/094–dc23
LC record available at https://lccn.loc.gov/2021001358
LC ebook record available at https://lccn.loc.gov/2021001359

Typeset by Hong Kong FIVE Workshop, Hong Kong
Print production managed by Jellyfish
Printed and bound by CPI Group (UK) Ltd, Croydon CR0 4YY

# CONTENTS

# ABOUT THE AUTHOR

After a 20-year career in corporate America, helping build the brands of global companies, services firms and non-profit organizations, Lida Citroën launched her firm, LIDA360, LLC in 2008. She set out to leverage her many years of experience helping global brands build, restructure and manage crisis in their reputation to now helping individuals. Her work as a reputation management and brand specialist is focused on facilitating international executives, professionals and entrepreneurs to position themselves more thoughtfully, pivot their reputation to new careers, and repair their image and reputation in complex marketplaces. Her clients come from every corner of the globe—from the United States to Spain to Poland, Argentina, Qatar, Singapore, Australia, Ireland and everywhere in between. She is internationally regarded as a leading authority on personal branding and positioning, online and in person.

As an award-winning speaker, keynote presenter and trainer, Citroën helps global audiences uncover the power of their narrative, find their compelling voice and value, and position themselves to a specific target audience. She routinely conducts in-person and virtual workshops, presentations and speeches for corporations, associations and non-profits, leveraging the personal branding message to align leaders with organizational values.

In 2011, Citroën published her first book, *Reputation 360: Creating power through personal branding*, which was immediately touted as a go-to guide for individuals looking to build and grow their reputation and brand.

In collaboration with LinkedIn Learning, Citroën created numerous instructional courses sharing aspects of personal branding and reputation management across multiple market sectors. Her courses range from "Creating Your Personal Brand" to "Repairing Your Reputation," "Having an Honest Career Conversation with Your Boss," "Reputation Risk Management," "Internal Interviewing" and others. Additionally, two of her courses are focused on veterans in career transition, and the employers who seek to hire them.

A civilian, Citroën has a deep personal passion for serving military veterans and has donated thousands of hours of coaching, writing and speaking to empower service members and veterans with the tools of personal branding to ensure their smooth and meaningful transition to the civilian sector. In 2015, Citroën published *Your Next Mission: A personal branding guide for the military-to-civilian transition*, which also gained attention from the human resources community which struggled to hire, onboard and retain former military. In 2016, her powerful TEDx Talk, "The power of gratitude and generosity—serving those who serve," brought attention to the important issues veterans face when leaving the military. In 2017, Citroën published her third book, *Engaging with Veteran Talent: A quick and practical guide to sourcing, hiring, onboarding and developing veteran employees*, a guide for human resources professionals seeking terminology, best practices and understanding of the military veteran job applicant. Citroën's fourth book, *Success After Service: How to take control of your job search and career after mil-itary duty* (Kogan Page, 2020), provides a comprehensive roadmap for service members readying to exit the military, and those who've separated recently. Full of examples, case studies and exercises, *Success After Service* released to great enthusiasm in the military community.

Citroën is featured often for her reputation management and personal branding work in leading media outlets, including the UK *Guardian*, Bloomberg, *New York Post*, *Handelsblatt*, MSNBC, CBN Television, US News, NBC News, Access Hollywood, Hallmark Channel, *Entrepreneur*, Military.com, *Military Times*, *CEO Magazine* and numerous other media, podcasts and websites.

She received her bachelor of arts degree in political science from Pomona College in Claremont, California, and is the recipient of several awards for her executive coaching work and community leadership.

# PREFACE

I grew up in Hollywood, California, an area known for being the entertainment capital of the world and where movies, television shows, celebrities and all things glittery come from. Everywhere around me were symbols of the glamour and mystique of the entertainment industry: Restaurant servers hoping to be discovered by talent scouts, celebrities signing autographs for adoring fans, and residents keeping up with the latest fashion trends to impress their neighbors. Many of my childhood friends were child actors, sometimes missing lessons or study hall to attend important acting auditions. Some even went on to become notable contributors to theater, film and television, leaving their mark in permanent and memorable ways. While I was not interested in a career in acting, later in life I'd realize how influential the entertainment industry would be on my career and life's work.

I attribute much of what I learned about managing reputation—from understanding how the optics of a situation influence beliefs, to crafting messaging and assessing the value of perception—to growing up in an environment focused on relevancy and image. If an actor's latest movie was a blockbuster success, they appeared on every talk show and radio program. They'd be photographed for the cover of magazines, could get seated at the best table at the best restaurants with no reservations, and the price for their performance in the next movie skyrocketed. They were considered a hot commodity by the powers that be. On the contrary, if a movie flopped, or a television show wasn't renewed, an actor could suffer long-term career challenges. There was also a risk called "becoming typecast," where an actor played a certain type of role (for example, a character in a long-running series or sequence of movies). If the role was successful, opportunities flowed. If not successful, opportunities could dry up and their reputation could be seen as too closely attached to the role they'd played which, in the minds of others, could be hard to disconnect from in future roles.

As a young adult, I recall dating a promising actor. Over dinner one night he said something that further shaped my perception of the industry and how it would apply to other careers as well. "As an actor, I spend my life playing the roles of other people," he told me. "In order to ever make a name for myself, I have to first pretend to be other people and get audiences to love me." Later, what struck me about his comment was that many professionals do the same thing outside of the entertainment industry: We believe that to be relevant and compelling we must first show up as other people, playing roles written by others, fulfilling expectations as we believe them to be, not necessarily as they are. What challenges this must bring, I thought.

As I grew my career in business, I encountered situations where I felt disingenuous and where I saw others acting in inauthentic ways. I saw people spending more than they could afford on clothing, jewelry and cars to impress others, professionals overstating their qualifications or professing to be passionate about a career path when they really weren't, and networking relationships that provided no substance and benefit, but were promoted as "rewarding" by one party. I was confused why I'd fall victim to behaving this way myself, feeling the pressure to be someone I wasn't and surrounding myself with people who acted the same way. Why were we all running at a pace that wasn't sustainable, trying to be someone we weren't, and failing to understand who we were and what we could offer the world and our community?

My career in the corporate arena spanned 20 years. I held titles of marketing director, business development executive, public relations specialist and branding expert. I was afforded wonderful opportunities to build, promote and scale some of the world's most notable and influential brands in industries such as consumer products, law, community investment, financial services and more. As I worked to amplify the brands and positioning of these companies and products, I found myself constantly coaching and guiding the front-line leadership team on their own positioning to ensure alignment with company goals. I was, in a way, helping to script their messaging for consistency with the values and objectives we promoted as a company, and they were, in fact, the actors in the process.

When the market crashed in 2008, many of us at the executive level found ourselves dusting off our résumés. I'd left a large non-profit organization where I'd led marketing, branding, public relations and positioning and I was tired of doing that work for big companies. A casual conversation with a colleague pointed out that what I was truly passionate about was helping people build their brand. The light bulb went off and LIDA360 was born. In the first years of building the company, I realized how vital it was to build my own brand—after all, my name was in the name of the company. I promoted personal branding and reputation management services to an international audience of professionals and executives who, because of the state of the global market at the time, were desperately trying to keep their job, find a job or find a better job. Fortuitously, my business timing couldn't have been better.

Building a brand for myself and my business required I lean fully into the beliefs, processes and training I would share with others. When I tell a client this work is hard and emotional, I can speak from first-hand experience, having done my own branding work! I evaluated my values, took inventory of my current reputation and brand, and set my vision for the future. It was through this work that "gratitude" and "generosity" emerged as words I'd not only lived by, but through which I'd create the vision for my career going forward. It's no wonder, then, that in 2009, at a Denver Broncos football game, I learned of the situation veterans face as they transition from a career of military service and enter the civilian sector. At that game, on that chilly fall day right before Veterans Day, I discovered a community that would become a huge part of my professional and personal focus.

Since 2009, I've worked closely alongside military and government organizations, private companies, veterans' groups and individual service members who all sought to understand this concept of personal branding to gain competitive advantage and feel in control of the opportunities they attracted. I've spoken to thousands of transitioning service members and veterans about the civilian work experience and how to position themselves effectively, and have trained hundreds of hiring managers, recruiters and employment specialists on the value of hiring and developing veteran employees.

In the years since launching my company, I've learned many things about how personal branding works, why executives focus on stature to promote their image, how fragile reputations are and what we need to do as good consumers of information regarding how we judge others. Personal branding sets the individual on a path that is full of self-actualized discovery, intention and strategy about how, where, when and why to show up a certain way with a certain audience. Without this focus, opportunities and challenges feel random and abstract and individuals may feel powerless over their careers.

And, I've learned how reputations can be destroyed in the blink of an eye or the tap of a keystroke. I never actually considered, as I read the news and heard of business leaders' indiscretions, or someone's infractions that caused them to suffer reputation damage, how commonplace this crisis was. I knew there were two sides to every story yet assumed the person had done something wrong. Having since worked with many clients who've found themselves in this predicament, I know now that someone doesn't have to do something wrong to be accused publicly and face scrutiny that follows them the rest of their career. Most importantly, I've learned that judgment is real and normal and painful. We judge without thinking. We assume without knowing, and we can hurt without intending.

I've been fortunate to be very busy working in the field of personal branding, which I am extremely passionate about. Whether I'm speaking to an audience of business leaders, advising CEOs of global companies or leading workshops of recent college graduates, my work rarely feels like work. I am one of those people who truly loves what she does. I see clients and audiences experience the spark of realization that they can direct their reputation, gain control over their career, and be more intentional about the relationships they seek and commit to. I've helped some of the most remarkable entrepreneurs launch businesses that will positively change the world, helped professionals speak to their communities with more authenticity, humility and clarity than they ever had before, and received the heartfelt notes from service members, deployed in combat zones, who are inspired and confident because a book I wrote makes them feel empowered. To say I get to live my ideal career every day would be an understatement.

In writing this book, I share stories, lessons, experiences, best practices and tools gained over many years for you to learn from. When I describe a client scenario, I have changed their name and some of the irrelevant information to protect my client's identity. The work I do is often deeply personal and very confidential, and while their stories are important, their actual names are not. I'll also give you my own experiences in this book and won't hold back, because some of it wasn't easy, pretty or painless. Living a life of congruity with your values is a process of self-discovery, assessment and goal-setting. When done correctly, the rewards are plentiful. My hope is that you find your journey in the stories and methodology contained here and see how your life and career can be enriched by controlling the narrative as you build, pivot or repair your reputation.

# Introduction

*Why is reputation management needed? What happens if we leave reputation to chance? This chapter highlights the reason more business leaders are leaning to reputation management to control the narrative over who they are and what they value.*

> *"Everyone has a personal brand: By design or by default."*
> LIDA CITROËN

Olivia was a successful female executive in a growing company. She'd hired many new staff in the time she'd been in the leadership role and, admittedly, she often struggled to provide one-on-one direction to them. Regardless, during one particular year her team exceeded all sales expectations, so she rewarded them with a party at a local restaurant. She brought team members into town from around the country and many toasts, drinks and snacks were enjoyed. At one point in the evening, Olivia excused herself to use the restroom. As she closed the bathroom stall door, she heard two women enter the restroom. Olivia didn't think much of it until the first woman said, "So, have you gotten to know Olivia? I mean *really* know her?" Now, Olivia realized she was about to overhear a conversation about herself! She became quiet and listened further. "Yes," said the second woman, "I have. And who the heck does she think she is?!" At that moment, Olivia realized she was listening to two women on her team—one she had worked with for years, the other was hired about six months previously. As she continued to listen in, she learned that they considered her to be rude, non-collaborative and overly aggressive. Olivia always enjoyed working fast and making bold decisions for herself and her team, but what she realized in those moments, in that restroom, was that the way her team perceived her was very different from how she intended. She had a reputation challenge.

Olivia's story is one example of someone who thinks they're being perceived one way but is actually coming across differently. Sometimes this doesn't matter. Most of the time it does. Olivia later realized that there had been breakdowns in communication within her team; there were times they didn't support her ideas and actually defied her orders. Could these be the results of the misaligned perception, she wondered? She'd considered herself pretty self-aware and in touch with her emotions and behaviors, but she realized she'd neglected to consider how her interactions with others were creating a view of who she was and what she cared about.

Hopefully, most of us won't find ourselves in Olivia's situation. Hopefully we're mindful, intentional and focused about what we say, how we say it, who we interact with (online and in person) and the impact of our brand on others. If you are, this book is for you. Here, you'll learn how to create stronger definitions of your value, focus more intently on the audiences you seek to influence, and measure the results you're achieving. Your goal may be to learn how to be more attentive to your personal brand-building, so the reputation you have, which you enjoy and are proud of, is sustained and maintained. You may, however, be in the majority of the population who've not focused on these concepts, strategies and tactics before, and wonder if your potential is fully maximized. Are you getting all the results you desire? Do people see you and appreciate what you can offer? Are you being rewarded for the leadership and contributions you make? Most people find themselves wondering if building a personal brand that is intentional and deliberate could afford them a stronger reputation in the minds of the people they seek to inspire, influence and impact. If you're wondering this as well, this book is for you, too. Or, perhaps you grabbed this book because you made a public misstep or mistake which is proving costly to your career and reputation. Maybe you posted something online you regret, or you stepped over a boundary with a colleague, or perhaps you're the victim of gaslighting or a targeted attack and find yourself needing resources to regain your name and career. This book is also for you.

The tools, resources, ideas and guides presented here are not intended to be used individually. Instead, they work together to weave a narrative of a reputation that can withstand outside pressures and negative influences, that is authentic and strong under scrutiny and is sustainable over time.

## Why do personal branding and reputation management matter?

As I raised my two sons and they'd encounter a bully or rude comment from a classmate, I often told them, "It doesn't matter what other people think of you. What matters is what you believe in your heart." And I was half right: What's in your heart, what you believe about yourself, and your confidence are paramount. You should hold your head high and know that you are unique, valuable, loved and valued. But we learn, as we grow up, that other people's perceptions of us also matter. If your boss perceives you to be lazy and uncooperative, you could be passed over for promotion, not given the resources and tools you need, or even fired. Building an intentional personal brand means you are in front of perception, driving the process of reputation development using any and all available tools. The result is not always a guarantee because we can't truly control how others think and what they feel, but we have more available tools than many realize. Starting with what's in your heart and building to be able to influence how others will perceive you is the power of personal branding.

If you choose to leave to chance that others will see you in the way you desire, I believe you truly give away power. You afford others the ability to define you the way they want and that is troublesome. In the twenty-first-century workplace, competitive advantage is at an all-time high. The marketplace has shifted—no longer do we compete for attention, opportunity and relationships from people in the same office, company or city. Now, competition comes from across the globe and from individuals who can clearly and concisely communicate their value to a target audience that's looking for them. We're not competing off of résumés today; we're leveraging social media and digital capital to show our reach and influence, we're using targeted narrative to get noticed, our professional networks are advocating, endorsing and referring us, and we're focusing in on the specific problems our target audiences need solved (and then playing up the value of our ability to solve them) to get ahead of our competition.

## Remove the abstract and random from your career

Another advantage you'll gain as you build, shift or fix your reputation is a sense of intention and focus unlike anything you may have experienced previously. Many of my clients and audiences express feeling in control over their career path, the options and opportunities afforded them seem less abstract, and decisions made are less random. With focus and clarity, you will evaluate each step forward in the context of the reputation you desire and be empowered with the criteria and confidence to boldly take charge of your future. Removing the abstractness and randomness from your career might feel subtle, or it could be an earthshattering experience for you as you now see your choices for how they are meaningful to you, not just for the financial rewards they present. For example, imagine you are considering a career move and have a lucrative compensation package on your desk to sign and accept. On the surface, more money and better perks sound like a great reason to pursue a change. But what if the opportunity presenting itself actually conflicts with your core values, presents challenges to your personal goals or could jeopardize your reputation because the company is not thought of favorably? Would the financial rewards be worth that risk? Your personal brand strategy and plan will give you the criteria to evaluate risk and reward, mitigating threat and ensuring you can measure and monitor results and effectiveness at every step.

## Why this book is needed now, more than ever before

As I'm writing this book, the world is in the midst of a global pandemic. Industries, economies and professionals around the globe are suddenly finding themselves pivoting, retooling, upskilling, reskilling, reimagining the future and struggling to keep up. Executives are working remotely from their home kitchen table instead of corporate suites, students are missing their friends, and entrepreneurs are wondering if the timing is right to take their idea to the investment community. Unlike anything in the past, the chaos and uncertainty of the future are impacting students, professionals, executives and entrepreneurs around the world. At the same time, companies are furloughing and shedding employees who are either unneeded in the current environment, who aren't worth investing in to upskill or retrain, or whose business line is suffering. Entire industries are laying off thousands of employees—from cruise line companies to airlines to hospitality to small businesses. The future of work is looking vastly different for many workers and business leaders.

Now, more than maybe ever before, the ability to be competitive and focused in your future career is vital. Today, executives must be thinking ahead, to a new and different future, where competition for visibility, credibility and opportunity will be heavy and mighty. While research and data reflecting the actual global impact of this shift from the pandemic are still to be developed, there are several indications (even anecdotally) we can look at to drive home this point:

- With businesses sending workers home to labor remotely, the "new normal" may mean you can live in Dubuque, Iowa, but report to a company based in San Jose, California. What will this mean for hiring and team development? Could this increase the available talent pool geographically and offer exponential opportunity for companies that may not have had a viable local workforce base to pull from?

- Work/life balance is being tested by workers at all levels. My executive clients tell me they are working much longer hours, have deferred any vacation, self-care and relaxation time, and their emotional and physical health is starting to suffer. Business leaders are pressured to calm and assuage the fears of their employees, even while questioning themselves whether the business will be able to withstand the economic impacts. This can lead to poor decision-making, strains on their personal life, and compromises of their values (and, therefore, their reputation).

- New businesses are springing up in response to these global changes. Not only are big companies retooling their machines and processes to respond to demand for things like face masks and hand sanitizer, but entrepreneurs are launching companies to meet new consumer demand. There are companies providing innovative face shields, "soap" for your mobile device to cleanse it of germs, and home delivery services are growing. Business leaders not paying attention to these innovations and trends could be leading their companies towards obsolescence.

- The world is connecting online more today. As global workers, business leaders and entrepreneurs were forced home to isolate during this time, the amount of online connection grew. A survey by GlobalWebIndex[1] reported that in July 2020 social media usage increased by 10.5 percent compared with the same time a year before. The report also found that people turned to social media engagement during the pandemic (46 percent of women and 41 percent of men), making it a highly popular activity online. As people around the globe found connection, support, information, news and entertainment online, the necessity for digital presence grew. To stand out, get noticed, be positioned as valuable and maintain their digital capital, savvy professionals needed to consider their online actions through the lens of their personal brands.

The good news is there are tools and resources available now to meet these needs. My work in personal branding and reputation management has always focused on a global audience, but I'm noticing more and more that professionals and executives from countries I'd have not considered interested in the past are seeking guidance. Business leaders around the world are looking to find their voice and power as they navigate the paradigm shift in their post-pandemic business and careers. Their issues, questions, concerns and dreams center around: How can I own my name and reputation? Can I create more meaning and impact in the work I do and the legacy I leave? What ways can I pull from my current brand to help me with my new career? How do I reclaim my name after an incident or situation damaged my reputation? How do I impact what someone finds when they Google my name?

## Who else should read this book?

In preparing this book, I intentionally focused on an executive audience. This is the audience I work most closely with, helping them build, pivot and repair their reputations. At the same time, others will surely be able to leverage the guidance and tools provided herein as I draw from experiences across many audiences and groups I've coached, clients who aren't in the executive ranks but whose situations map to those experienced by a senior business leader, and anecdotally from peers and colleagues who've shared their stories. I've also written the advice here to support:

- **College, university and graduate students**—As you start your career, this book will provide a roadmap of how to grow, manage and develop your reputation and career over time. Learn from the lessons shared by people more experienced than yourself. Their examples will highlight how you can chart a path forward that is rewarding, meaningful and impactful, and will show the landmines to avoid. I remember being hired by the sorority of a university to deliver a lecture on personal branding, reputation strategies and the risks of social media. We discussed what to post, what to avoid, and how to filter decisions through the question of whether or not sharing that comment, post, image or video would advance their reputation or could hurt them. The audience of 200 college-aged women took copious notes. I can't help but imagine they avoided costly mistakes because their awareness about the impact of social media on their reputation and careers was strengthened that day.

- **Parents returning to work after an absence**—Whether you stepped out of the workforce for maternity or paternity leave, or to care for a spouse or parent, returning to work and re-establishing credibility can be challenging. The workplace may have shifted, your skills might need fine-tuning, and your team may have grown in unanticipated ways. How will you establish your value, reclaim your authority and position yourself to be aligned with the reputation you seek, maybe not the one you had before? These issues are certainly addressed in this book.

- **Professionals and entrepreneurs who want their stories told**— Many professionals and business owners are concerned that their narrative isn't being told the way they want. They're worried that over time the way they are depicted or regarded isn't in alignment with their work or passion and they turn to personal branding solutions to rectify their situation. When coming from the clarity and vision of who they are today compared with how they want to be perceived, having a plan to achieve reputation that is desirable, and systems to monitor results, they feel in control over the narrative about their life and work that resembles their ideal. Even professionals just starting out, and entrepreneurs at the infancy stage of their company or product launch, benefit from considering the end goal (desired brand) and working backwards to ensure consistency and traction are achieved in building their reputation.

- **Individuals seeking to impact global concerns and communities**— Online platforms and tools today allow people to connect with, support and promote issues and causes in all corners of the planet. As they seek to increase the visibility and credibility of their initiative or population, some individuals will want to use the tools, ideas and examples presented here to build up their reputation and support their life's work.

- **People who seek to integrate their interests, hobbies and side hustles into one narrative**—Many people today work side jobs or have interests outside of work that support their career. The "gig economy" is growing as businesses like Uber, pet walking, network marketing, freelance consulting and others offer people the chance to earn extra income and are growing in popularity. These businesses and jobs offer flexible schedules and income for people seeking diversity of work, extra money and benefits. The question most commonly asked is, "How do I weave that type of work into my overall career narrative?" Choosing how, where and why to include side work or hobbies into your online profiles, professional résumé and other career tools is answered through discovery of your positioning and brand strategy.

## Why I wrote this book

When I approached my publisher with the idea for this book, I'd already spent years capturing ideas, case studies and notes in a folder. I had scraps of paper with one word on them, and reams of journals with ideas and examples outlined in great detail. As I'd worked with clients over the past decade plus, I knew their stories were unique and special, but they could also serve to help and influence others who were likely in a similar spot or on the same journey. In 2011, I wrote and published my first book, *Reputation 360: Creating power through personal branding*, and felt confident at the time that anyone reading it could easily walk through their personal branding journey to a successful outcome. I remember thinking at the time that I'd left nothing on the cutting-room floor—no idea, tip, resource or suggestion had been omitted, so the book would serve to be a complete guide to building career control through personal branding. And it did just that. Readers loved it, benefited from it, and generously shared their success stories with me over the years. But I knew that the time was right for a more elevated look at reputation management and controlling narrative.

Also, now I have more to say. I've worked complex and intricate reputation-building strategies with global business leaders, triaged reputation crises for high-profile clients, and guided the personal brand-building and reputation design with some of the most fascinating people around the world. They might not be household names to you, but they are leaders in their fields, companies, industries and communities. I knew the work we did would benefit others who need to learn from them. I also feel it is important to elevate many of the topics around reputation management which, over time, have been commoditized. The field of personal branding and reputation management has been flooded with consultants, coaches and speakers from differing backgrounds and with differing levels of experience. I felt it important to bring a more executive approach to the process for the benefit of practitioners as well as executives, to help the industry stay focused on the end result: to live a fulfilled, meaningful and purposeful career through control over the way we are perceived. If I can achieve that goal, my legacy will be positively impacted.

## How to read this book

Sometimes you're not ready. Sometimes your reputation isn't ready. But when you and your reputation are ready, the unfolding of perfectly timed events seems almost magical. I've met many clients who tried to launch a business before establishing a value proposition for the company. Or clients who tried to move on after a reputation crisis, believing that their online followers would just "get over it" and forget what happened. And clients who've tried to prematurely speak their truth to audiences who weren't ready to hear their message. In cases where this happens, it doesn't mean the company or message is wrong, it just might be ill timed or too soon.

In this book we'll review timing and the cadence through which you'll bring others along with you in understanding who you are, what you value, and why offering this value to others is meaningful to you and them. There's a timing element which is crucial to unveiling your personal brand, pivoting your brand or repairing your reputation. The steps are vital, and the timing ensures the foundation of your communication is solid, the strategy is vetted, and the tactics are clear to build and monitor results. I recall early in my new business I set up a vibrant and content-rich online offer that I was sure would result in wonderful residual income. With the help of a friend whose expertise was in the web/e-commerce space, I created several modules of content that offered professionals the ability to self-pace their learning and build their brands from the comfort of their own home and computer. The content was solid, the design was beautiful, but the project failed. I realized later that the project failed because the one thing I didn't have (yet) was notoriety as an expert on the topic. I was known to my friends, clients, previous coworkers and some online circles, but I had yet to achieve the visibility and success I needed to drive audiences to this site. Later, in working with the team at Lynda.com (which later became LinkedIn Learning), I also realized there was much to learn about the development of online content which I had naively believed I could do without more skills. All in all, learning and credibility made my later ventures into the online course field much more successful.

Whether you like to move fast through content, or you prefer a more slow-paced learning, you'll find the structure of this book works well. I've enjoyed working with clients who like to move swiftly, who revel in seeing perception shift in large ways in short order. I've equally appreciated the patience of other clients who recognized that what got them where they are wasn't quick and they work the process slowly to build long-term success. In this book, you'll hear from both types of clients. Taking shortcuts, looking for quick-fixes and rounding corners too abruptly can actually create more damage than doing nothing at all. In the case of reputation repair, for instance, I recall a man named Albert, who had been publicly accused of an affair with a minor. His marriage was in shambles, his adult children refused to speak to him, and his work as a management consultant was in jeopardy. As his employer decided whether the heat from the headlines was too hot for them to be comfortable supporting their executive, Albert impulsively made a public statement to the media (via Twitter). He shared: "I did not have an affair with an underage girl. The allegations are false. She was 18 years old at the time we met. And, even if I did, I thought 'love is love', right? Who cares?!" And he was immediately fired. His lapse of judgment, his indiscretion and the casual way he addressed his situation resulted in his employer, friends and professional colleagues immediately distancing themselves from him. Timing does matter. But more importantly, the steps to repair reputation—whether you did something to warrant the damage or not—must be followed to avoid additional costly mistakes.

## Be prepared to get uncomfortable

In the course of reading this book, you will undoubtedly feel uncomfortable. Perhaps you'll realize, as Olivia did in the opening of this chapter, that what you thought you were doing right was creating a contrary positioning for yourself. Maybe in the discussion we'll have about values you'll realize that much of what you deemed important and where you assigned your personal and spiritual values is now in question. Possibly the idea of envisioning the end of your life in order to establish your desired legacy brings up feelings that make you overwhelmingly sad.

As you consider the questions and concepts posed in this book, allow yourself to go even farther outside of your comfort zone. Ask yourself:

· When do I feel most powerful and confident?

· When did I feel most proud of my actions?

· What am I most grateful for?

· If I wasn't afraid, what would I do?

· When do I feel like my true self? And, when do I feel most censored?

The answers might surprise, delight, upset or alarm you. That's okay! As you learn more about yourself, your motivations and your goals, you'll experience feelings of intention and control like never before. You'll discover why the power of the inside–out process reveals opportunity to stretch and grow your knowledge, relationships and contribution. You might also elect to read through the book first, skipping the exercises the first time through and committing to going back and completing them later.

Another approach to reading the book might be to read a chapter and then reflect on your feelings, ideas or reactions, capturing them in a journal to review later. This process could uncover your biases, preconceived ideas or misconceptions that have guided you and your career up until this point. By capturing them on paper in real time, you'll be able to tangibly see your process of thinking evolve to a new level of insight, perspective and consideration that will serve you going forward.

## Acknowledgments

Finally, I could not be here with all of the years of experience, stories, opportunities and challenges without the wonderful clients who've trusted me to guide their reputation journeys. These clients have come from all walks of life, industries and countries around the globe. With each new engagement and project, I've learned more about people than I could have imagined: What makes them happy, excited, fulfilled and what leads them to serve when the odds are not in their favor. I've seen courageous individuals give up their careers, income and networks to pursue work that has a greater social impact. I've helped clients lean farther into their passion than they thought possible and reap the benefits and rewards. I've helped clients with horror stories of reputations attacked from online trolls, and where gaslighting has led even a confident and successful professional to question everything about their life and livelihood. And I've seen careers shattered and rebuilt by brave individuals who had the faith, resilience and tenacity to see that their story was retold the way they wanted. Whether building, pivoting or repairing reputation, my clients have shown me their strength, humor, compassion and toughness in the process. I'm truly grateful for the experience of knowing each and every one of them.

I've benefited from learning and growth at the hands of many professional colleagues who've been generous enough to share their feedback, insights, best practices and learning with me along the way. As an entrepreneur, there was much I didn't know when I started this journey, and through informal mentoring and conversations, I was helped by many.

I want to expressly thank the team at Kogan Page, my publishers. Their collaborative approach and professionalism have made the experience of writing books a true joy! My team at LIDA360 has been patient, knowledgeable and resilient as I've taken them on the journey of building a company and serving clients around the world. Thank you for your hard work and friendship.

And my family and friends—thank you for being on this crazy and wonderful ride with me. Scott, Eileen, Clark, Beau and Grace: You've helped me see the possibilities when I was head-down in the fog, you've reminded me of the values I set forth, held me accountable to living my life and career fully and authentically, and shown me how I could control the narrative of my life and legacy. I love you all dearly.

## Endnote

1  Globalwebindex.com (2020) Coronavirus Research Hub: The Latest On Global Consumer Impact, https://www.globalwebindex.com/coronavirus (archived at https://perma.cc/VF9F-LBSS)

# 01

# How perception is formed

*Here, you'll understand how impression, perception and reputation are formed and why they drive beliefs. With examples of how perception works, we'll examine what happens when we leave impression to chance.*

What happens when we see someone walking towards us? Maybe we don't notice, oblivious to their presence. But what if that person is walking towards us late at night and we're in a dark alley in an unfamiliar part of town? Then, we're likely to notice them and quickly create beliefs about who they are, what they need or want, and whether they want to harm us.

Judgment and perception are traits that humans share with animals. These traits allow us to assess for danger and threat (saber-toothed tiger approaching!) and opportunities (they look friendly—we could be friends!). They draw us towards people we may want to be in a relationship with, who align with our values and goals, and keep us from getting too close to others who might want to hurt us. Understanding how perception is formed and why we judge is important to building a personal brand and reputation management strategy. Here, we'll look at both the neuroscience of how we form impressions and stereotypes and the conditioned habits of judgment and culture that play into our perception of others.

By understanding our biology and conditioning, we can understand what we have control over, which variables we can influence and manipulate, and which ones need to be acknowledged and understood to work through. Where there is science to back the assertions, I will cite it. Where the information and assessments are anecdotal, I'll note that, too. We've all had experience with perception—we quickly form an impression and tell ourselves a story about who that person is, what they value, and where they come from. We may even believe we can know their intention or thoughts. Often, we aren't proud of those stories, because they include biases and stereotypes that highlight our naiveté. But we do this... and others do this too. Navigating, overcoming and working through the bias of others will be featured in later chapters.

## Perception is not an absolute

Has this happened to you? You hire someone you think will do a great job. In the job interview, they were charismatic, personable and sold themselves and their skills brilliantly. But once in the job, the wheels fall off and they seem to be completely incompetent at what you hired them to do. Author Gregory Berns states in his book, *Iconoclast*,[1] "Perception is the brain's way of interpreting ambiguous visual signals in the most likely explanation possible. These explanations are a direct result of past experience." We use the patterns of our past to draw conclusions about what we see today, and your personal brand will live within, and work through, your perceptions of the world, and other people's perception of you. When thinking about a person we both know, we might imagine that our beliefs and perceptions of that person would be similar—after all, we both know them. Yet, each of us brings our own emotional filters, beliefs, ideas and views of what we're seeing and experiencing. This colors how we perceive the person standing in front of us.

There are also differences we'll focus on based on what we value. Because of my upbringing, culture and personal belief system, I might place high value on intelligence and knowledge. Then, when I see our mutual friend reading or delivering a thoughtful talk, I deem them "smart and forward-thinking." Based on your upbringing, culture and personal beliefs, you might value connectivity and inclusiveness and might see our friend as "standoffish and aloof" because they are sitting apart from others and not engaging with them.

## Unconscious bias

Biases come in many forms. Unconscious bias shows up in subconscious ways when we assign credibility (or lack thereof), threat, beliefs and positive attributes to something new, based on what's happened in the past. "Unconscious biases are social stereotypes about certain groups of people that individuals form outside their own conscious awareness. Everyone holds unconscious beliefs about various social and identity groups, and these biases stem from one's tendency to organize social worlds by categorizing."[2] While sometimes harmless (such as when someone with the same name reminds you of a childhood friend you remember fondly), often it's unconscious bias that leads to racism, sexual discrimination, ageism and other prejudices that directly harm others. Employers for decades have brought unconscious bias into the hiring process of military veterans, for instance. Their belief that anyone who served in the military or saw combat must have anger issues, PTSD and other behavioral issues has been remedied through training and awareness.

Still today, however, unconscious bias shows up in how we feel and react when confronted with news of a business leader caught cheating on their taxes ("of course they cheat, otherwise how could they make all that money?") or a celebrity marrying another celebrity ("pretty people marry other pretty people") or a star student performing well ("people from that country are always good at math") or why we believe certain politicians over others ("he served in Congress a long time; he'd never lie"). When unconscious bias prevents us from seeing the situation or individual clearly, or when it directs us forward without all the information, we're at a disadvantage and the bias is preventing us from success.

## Confirmation bias

Confirmation bias is a tricky form of emotional filtering and often directs our ability to judge a situation, event or person. With this bias, we purposefully seek out information, experiences and relationships that confirm our beliefs, often ignoring valuable data that could serve us. When someone leads with confirmation bias, we may think of them as "narrow-minded" or having a "one-track mind." They seem to reject any conversation that doesn't support their theories or ideas. This person rejects additional information—particularly contrasting data—and then makes decisions based on this bias.

An example of confirmation bias: A business owner believes that workers with college degrees are smarter and more valuable to the company than their peers who did not complete their degree. The owner promotes and advances those employees who have degrees, keeping non-degreed employees focused on less attractive work. As the degreed employees ascend into leadership roles, the owner affirms that it's their commitment to education and learning that helped them succeed. When a non-degreed employee applies for, and is considered for, a management role, the owner puts more scrutiny on their credentials and interview than the degreed employee. Often, the level of scrutiny and "higher bar" eliminates the non-degreed employee, even if they could have been a great asset to the management team.

Confirmation bias leads us to seek out people who believe the same as us. We connect with them on social media, follow them in the news, and share their insights with "non-believers" around us. Confirmation bias is popular during times of stress and struggle as people search for evidence that their theories around global crisis, political injustice, social conflict, etc. are justified and warranted. When someone's default processing runs through negative emotional filters and they operate out of negative confirmation bias, there are ways to correct this if they are aware of the problem. Being mindful that these tendencies are driving decision-making and behavior allows the individual to modify them. The tendency may always exist—it can be hard to break the chains of long-standing beliefs—but behavior modification specialists have proven that rewiring negative thinking can lead to redesigning behavior.

## Personal branding lives through perception, judgment, beliefs and trust

Key to any personal brand strategy is understanding how perception, judgment, belief and trust work independently, and together, to influence reputation. When managing perception, if we can understand and influence the judgment our target audience might have of us and build credibility and trust with them, reputation thrives. If we aren't aware of the perceptions others have of us, or if there is a lack of credibility around what we stand for and promote, it's easy for our reputation to succumb to unreasonable scrutiny and fractures.

Examples of managing perception and influencing judgment include: The individual who makes an off-handed comment on Twitter and suddenly finds themselves the center of a hostile online discussion about race relations; or the doctor who gets fired from a high-profile position after indiscretion with a patient and who has NOT paid attention to personal brand strategies—they can find themselves trying to remove incoming water from a fast-filling rowboat using a teaspoon. Their efforts may be futile at best.

## Optics matter

You may have heard it said about the media, high-profile lawsuits or politics that the goal is to "control the optics." The idea here is that when you can control what people see, you'll control how they feel and their perception about what they're looking at. Optics typically describes what we're looking at. Politicians have long recognized that to appeal to their constituents (voters and prospective voters), they have to appear a certain way: likable, relatable, charismatic, knowledgeable, etc. In the 1960 presidential election campaign, Richard Nixon and John F. Kennedy were tasked with holding one of their first televised election debates. Nixon had recently been released from the hospital following a knee injury and had actually reinjured the same knee en route to the debate. Refusing to reschedule the event,

Nixon looked pained and sickly during the debate. Kennedy's team opted to improve his appearance with the use of makeup and styling. Nixon, on the other hand, refused to be "touched up" to look better on camera. Seventy million television viewers watched a confident and tan Kennedy outshine a pale and sick-looking Nixon in responding to the debate questions. Kennedy's appearance is said to have greatly influenced the way voters perceived him and his debate performance: healthy, vibrant, confident and ready for the job. Optics matter.

In business, leaders seek to appeal to their stakeholders—employees, management team, board of directors, investors, etc.—similarly. "How do they need to see me and how can I show up that way?" is routinely considered when seeking to influence and impact a target audience. The CEO has to deliver bad news to the company? They should look solemn and upset, maybe in a less than polished suit (implying they have been staying up late at night trying to rectify the situation). When the CFO is delivering quarterly earnings reports to shareholders, they need to appear confident, rested and excited about the future. Optics, along with a good idea, drive the message home.

Gwen is a client of mine who's a leader in healthcare. She has spent her education and entire career focused on helping patients reform their lives after weight loss surgery. Gwen knows this audience well—she's studied them, spent countless hours with them, writes articles and delivers speeches to help them. When considering how Gwen would look for an upcoming photo shoot to promote her new book and website, we thought hard about how she would appear: "I can't look skinny or too confident," she shared. This audience needed to see her as relatable, someone who understood what it means to live with obesity and want to change their life. "I want to look like who they aspire to be," Gwen continued. "And that person isn't a supermodel. Just a real person who lives a healthy lifestyle." The optics of how she presented herself were critical to building a relationship with this audience and making sure her message was received.

# Perception

## *Perception as reality*

How many times have we heard the statement "perception is reality"? What someone believes to be true feels real to them, the way they see it and experience it. The frustrating aspect of this understanding is that perception can be very subjective; yet if you understand how perceptions are formed you can affect and help trigger specific responses that are favorable to you. Someone's belief about you (or perception of you) does not make it, in fact, real, but it can feel or appear real to them. As we interpret the world around us and form beliefs to confirm, understand or refute what we see and experience, we may interpret our conclusions as "real" when they are actually perceived.

Perception drives our approach to the world around us. If we perceive opportunities to be flourishing, we'll greet each encounter with optimism and joy. If we perceive the world to be a hateful and dangerous place, we will fear forming relationships with people different from us, will resist helping others and may choose not to contribute to society in meaningful ways.

## *How perceptions are shaped: The neuroscience*

Research into how perception is formed is wide and deep. Neuroscience research reveals how our eyes interpret competing data and stimuli, how social stereotypes impact decision-making, and why certain images are considered threatening and others pleasing. Taken altogether, the research provides evidence that we form perception based on conscious and subconscious stimuli or "triggers."

Here's how this works: To receive information, one or more of our five senses picks up an external stimulus. We smell it, see it, touch it, hear it or taste it, and begin to experience it. Our senses send information to our brain telling us something about that stimulus and our brain begins to organize the information into patterns that help us make sense out of what we're experiencing. Then, the new information that's now organized is measured and evaluated against other experiences and information we have, familiar aspects are identified, and our brain tells us what's happening—what this new information means and how we should react or respond.

It is the stage of interpreting the new information where biases, emotional filters and other human behaviors influence perception. As our sensory organs send information to the brain, and we organize and interpret what we're seeing, tasting, feeling, hearing or touching, we filter the experience through what we've already felt, have been taught about that experience, or what we believe to be true about those types of experiences. As a child, as you reached for the hot stove you were either told by someone (likely an adult) "don't touch that!" or you saw someone else shriek after touching a hot stove and you remembered long enough to resist the temptation to touch the stove. Or, you touched it and were burned, storing that information for when temptation strikes again. Our familiarity with similar experiences guides our thinking and assessment of what this is and how we should feel about it: That sound seems like a scream for help. That sound seems like a scream of joy. That smell is delightful and pleasing. That smell is terrible.

It is reasonable to believe that unless you have certain knowledge about a stimulus, you might not know how to respond to it or what to feel about it. Our ability to discern, evaluate, deliberate and draw perceptions makes us unique among species. We don't always just react on instinct; we consider and decide. While the initial act of experiencing the stimulus may be unconscious, and the formation of our perception of that stimulus is also unconscious, soon we begin to interpret and form an understanding and belief about what we're experiencing. It is at this stage that we do something as a direct response to what we perceive to be happening.

EXPECTATION IMPACTS PERCEPTION

But what happens when there's a disconnect between what we see, what we expect to see or what we believe we're seeing?

- What happens when what we expect to see is different from what our brain registers as being in our view?

- What happens when an incomplete picture is presented, yet we interpret that the entire image is present?

- Why are some images pleasing to the eye and others abhorrent? And why does pleasure/displeasure vary between viewers so much?

If perception is heavily influenced by what we know and believe, what happens when we expect to see something in advance of what we experience? Does expectation influence what we perceive and how "real" we believe it to be? Professor Dr. Albert Newen from the Institute for Philosophy II offers this explanation: "A chess expert would see the chessboard in a different way than a beginner, because he activates relevant structured patterns automatically as background knowledge, and that knowledge affects the perception process. This also takes place during social perception of other people."[3]

Many researchers have run experiments showing subjects part of an image—the outline of a face or of a body, for instance—and watched how they perceived the image as complete. Images of garbled letters show up on social media with the claim, "If you can read this, you're a genius!" Know that our mind will unscramble basic, familiar words to make sense of them. But sometimes when expectations—and our natural tendency to fill-in-the-blanks on what we're seeing—don't actually present a complete or real picture, we're left with a distorted view and struggle to form perception. Someone sees the homeless man running from the crime scene and perceives he is the assailant, instead of asking whether he was also a victim, or was running to get help. What we expect to see in others can greatly distort the reality we perceive to be true.

As the neuroscience indicates, "The ability to quickly perceive emotion patterns based on the facial expression and body language of another person is crucial for social animals like humans."[4] We will explore this more when we consider how image, behavior and body language directly create and drive perception and reputation.

### EXTERNAL INFLUENCES DRIVE PERCEPTION

Your parents may have told you rich people were greedy. Your news media tell you ethnic people are dangerous. Your culture supports the belief that women should not work outside the home. Your friends gossip that Sally isn't to be trusted with your boyfriend. Daily, we are bombarded with cues and messages—on television, online, in conversation—about what to believe, how to think and when to judge. Often, separating fact from fiction, stereotype from truth and perception from reality takes awareness, commitment and skill.

### CULTURE INFLUENCES PERCEPTION

Cultures unite us around common beliefs, behaviors and communication to ensure the sanctity and sustainability of the cultural values. Cultural codes are both overt and subtle, grounded in tradition and history and practiced in person and online. These codes often play as "tapes" reminding members of the culture what is expected of them, how to behave, and what to value. How you were raised, who raised you and the culture in which you grew up can also strongly influence how you perceive the world. Later, in our discussion of values, you will see further how culture can shape what you believe, what you value, how you make decisions, and how optimistic you are about your future. Even cultures such as that in the military create perceptions of what is honorable, who is to be respected, and what constitutes valor. After leaving the military, many veterans still carry these beliefs with them long after they've left active duty.

In perception management we recognize that cultures "are powerful propagators of information and are shaped by the values and ideas promoted within. The culture that you come from can shape your personal attention style, memory and emotions."[5] Cultures teach us what is to be believed and who is to be trusted. Our cultural norms are often hard-wired into our way of thinking, making it hard for the individual to separate the two.

In her book, *Creating We*, Judith E. Glaser notes, "In Eastern cultures, communities tend to find identity in their shared culture. Alternatively, in the West, the individual is sent inward to search for an identity and fulfill their 'destiny' through the discovery and pursuit of a life passion/purpose."[6] Within the culture, we feel comfortable and safe. In the military, where everyone swears to uphold the same values, service members feel a unity and camaraderie that's reassuring and consistent. The artist who seeks self-expression and untethered creativity might feel more at home in a community with a free-spirited culture, where they'd feel supported.

Two such examples of cultural codes or drivers are Tall Poppy Syndrome and FIGJAM, both memorable beliefs which impact self-promotion and branding. My clients from the United Kingdom and Australia often remind me of Tall Poppy Syndrome as a cultural belief, and how it impacts their behavior, attitude and willingness to promote themselves. Tall Poppy Syndrome refers to how poppies naturally should grow: together. One should not stand out, be taller or more prominent than the others. If one grows more conspicuous, it should be cut down to size, humbled and depreciated to bring it into alignment with the others. "That's how it should be," clients tell me. This "syndrome" causes clients from these cultures to be reluctant to self-promote, to self-congratulate and to advance their own brand among their peers.

Similarly, FIGJAM refers to the negativity associated with self-promotion. I remember the first time a prominent executive client from Sydney used this expression with me to explain his reluctance to build up his social media presence. He didn't want to appear boastful, arrogant or immodest. FIGJAM, he explained, is a common expression in Australia, standing for "F**k. I.'m G.ood, J.ust A.sk M.e." It's often used to describe those individuals who boast excessively after completing a task or project, who draw attention to themselves unnecessarily and who thrive on attention.

Culturally, beliefs like these become part of our perception matrix. We evaluate our own behaviors through them, and critique and decide how we feel about others using these metrics. Someone seems too proud of their successes. They suffer from Tall Poppy Syndrome. A colleague announces his promotion on social media. FIGJAM comes to mind, and so on.

### SOCIAL MEDIA INFLUENCES PERCEPTION

To list the many ways social media influences, drives and creates perception would fill volumes. We have all seen evidence of group think, mob and crowd mentality online, maybe even succumbing to social pressure and chiming in ourselves. It's natural that online we gravitate towards like-minded individuals and often are intrigued and attracted to differing opinions, thoughts and experiences. The online space makes it easier and more accessible to connect with those who are different from us, as well as those we're like, even offering the option of remaining anonymous as we do so.

Evidence of the impact of social media in driving perception occurs constantly: Influencers on Instagram are paid handsomely by advertisers for the number of followers and "likes" they attract. While the average follower may intuitively know their celebrity crush is being paid to promote a product, their perception of that product—when attached to someone they admire and revere so highly—rises exponentially. Ultimately, this drives sales.

Causes, issues, companies, products all rely on the power of perception. For 20 years I worked in corporate America, helping to build the brands of global leaders in professional services, consumer products and financial instruments. Our goal was to drive a narrative and create perception in our favor. Before we could market and promote our service or product, we had to create a belief system around our product, service or company, and ensure our target market saw the value in what we had to offer. Perception around what we sold didn't happen by accident; it was well designed.

Social media is supposed to be user-generated content, shared in the open social sphere. Today, there is pressure to return social media to being more of a natural exchange of ideas rather than a corporate sponsor-managed machine that pushes a specific perception around elections, consumer behavior and credibility of individuals. Consider what happens when the CEO of a well-respected company makes an ill-advised post online. Whether from ignorance, anger, laziness or exhaustion, they post something they later regret. Whether it is a poorly phrased sentiment, an inappropriate photo, or a joke that lands wrong, the online community can quickly and aggressively attack this person's character and what they stand for. They can create a mob to attack them with harsh comments and memes, boycott their company and even threaten their family's safety. The online community, often with very little context, can destroy a person and their company quickly and ruthlessly. Negative perception, in this case, spreads like fire.

## TRADITIONAL MEDIA INFLUENCES PERCEPTION

Traditional media is the news, magazines and radio outlets created to communicate what is happening locally, nationally and globally. Originally, news outlets adhered to strict boundaries set by the profession of journalism that required they report what was occurring without commentary or opinion (theirs or their employer's). The field of journalism has broadened, encompassing media outlets that range from local coverage of news events to national political punditry. The line between news reporting and opinion has blurred. The media format itself likely changed first: Traditional media started as one-way communication. Journalists reported the news, we watched, learned, discussed with family and friends, and formed perceptions about what we heard. Social media opened up a dialog, offering viewers the chance to share their views, opinions and knowledge with the journalists themselves, and with other viewers. This changed the dynamic greatly.

As the format shifted, the door was opened for more opinion-based commentary in those traditional media outlets. Soon, editorializing was not relegated to the end of the broadcast but woven throughout the news delivery. For many viewers, this became confusing as they couldn't delineate between the facts of what was being reported (Person X robbed a bank) and opinion (Person X was a bad person, growing up in a poor part of town, which explains why they robbed the bank).

What is shown on the newscast, what is left out? Who is interviewed as an expert, who isn't invited to comment on the topic? Producers consider what the reporter should wear, how they'll sit on the couch for the interview and other subtleties for their effect and impact on the message. Even the inflection in a journalist's voice as they share their concern over what's happening on the screen sends a specific and intentional message. Each of these choices, and others, can directly influence the conclusion (perception) the viewer makes about the content they are consuming.

As today's traditional news media confidently and unapologetically takes a stand on a topic, branding levers have had to adjust. In the past, a well-placed press release, a timely press conference or letter to the editor could help calm public perception on an issue before it spiraled out of control. Today, business leaders must contend with new, sometimes more unpredictable allies and foes in the media.

*Can we modify or manipulate perception?*

When I teach personal branding strategies to audiences of professionals, I'm often asked if we can manipulate or influence the perceptions other people have of us. Yes, I reply, I believe we can. While we can't control other people or force them to feel or believe something (they might tell us they believe it, but we can't force their beliefs), we can influence their thinking and the way they perceive, and form judgments as a result. Using strategic narrative, managing the optics and building promotional campaigns, we can change the way a politician appears to their constituents, a celebrity aligns with a new character, and a business tycoon has learned from their mistakes. Careful calculation, intentional and thoughtful narrative and promotion can certainly influence (positively or negatively) the way others see them. This happens every day.

# Judgment

*What is judgment?*

As we form perceptions about what we're experiencing (feeling, seeing, touching, hearing, tasting), we assess situations, people, projects and our environment using emotional filters. These tools often lead us to prematurely form judgments about our experience. An emotional filter is a sort of lens through which you view new information, but because it is only based on what you have previously experienced and formed opinions about, these filters can significantly tighten the aperture of your reasoning and view of how the world works.

Here's an example of how this works: If I was attacked by a dog as a child, I might believe all dogs are threatening. When my neighbor introduces their new puppy to me, I'm frightened and see the dog as bad and lash out. I've judged her new dog based on my experiences. Another example: If teachers in school repeatedly told me that I'd never amount to anything and was not capable of success, I might question and challenge my boss wanting to promote me to management. I'd have internalized that message of low worth and feel that anyone who thought I was worthy of leadership opportunities was obviously flawed in their assessment of me. While it is certainly healthy for our minds to filter out bad thoughts and help us respond and react to good thoughts, if our filters are based on misinformation, or trauma, they can lead us astray.

### Different types of judgment

If you're like me, you were raised with the belief that "judging" people is wrong. We aren't supposed to hastily form beliefs about other people based on what they look like, sound like or how they interact with us—how could we possibly know their whole story? But we do judge, constantly: She looks smart, he seems pushy, she doesn't like her boss, he should NOT be wearing that... One problem with judgment is there is so much interpretation between what I see (and then process) and what you see (and then process) before we judge. Judgment is, by definition, subjective. For example, I see a young woman stopping to help a man with directions. You say she's naïve—that stranger could be trying to scam or hurt her! She should know better. Dumb blonde. I see someone helping another person and being generous with her time. I smile as I watch her, you shake your head.

Another problem with judgment is we have such limited context in which to form judgment. In the situation described above, neither I nor you know why the woman was helping the stranger, whether she ended up being scammed or whether she was a nice person. We have very limited context in which to judge others (this point will become very important later in this book!).

There are different ways we judge, as well.

- **Moral judgment** refers to "the determination a person makes about an action (or inaction), motive, situation, or person in relation to standards of goodness or rightness. People articulate a moral judgment, for example, when they say that an action is right or wrong, that a person is good or bad, or that a situation is just or unjust."[7] When we say someone is honest, genuine, sincere and can be trusted, we are making moral judgments.

- **Social judgment** refers to our judgment of someone in the way they relate to others. Are they friendly, likable, generous, kind? Do they give of themselves to help others?

- **Competence judgment** happens when we judge someone's capabilities. Do we think they can get the job done? Will they be able to meet their own goals? When we judge someone on their skills, intelligence, knowledge and abilities, we're judging them on competence:

    It's not just that people want to *know* about a person's moral character.
    When we do learn about a person's honesty and trustworthiness,
    it factors into our opinions of them more than other information.
    Several studies have shown this to be the case.[8]

## Judgment scares us (and yet we crave it)

Social media changed how we judge. Some would argue it's changed it for the worse. On social media and in online networking, all we do is judge. We "like" posts we agree with, find entertaining or want to support. We "love" posts, comments and images we REALLY agree with and feel strongly about. And, we add a frowny-face emoji to things we find distasteful or disagreeable. Beyond this, we may even add our opinion and fact-check or argue against content we don't like. We are constantly—almost instinctively—drawn to add judgment to everything we see on social networking sites like Facebook, Instagram, Twitter, LinkedIn and more.

Likely judgment scares us because it reveals our own vulnerability to being judged. When we judge others, we put on a defensive mask of "I can pick apart your value first, before you do it to me." It is argued we judge because we fear being judged. The popular statement, "You'll worry less about what people think about you when you realize how seldom they do,"[9] has been attributed to many individuals and highlights our belief that others are constantly thinking about us, judging us, talking behind our backs—and when we imagine this happening, we rarely consider it to be a positive thing. It's like we imagine them all speaking ill of us, and criticizing our values, actions, wardrobe or lifestyle choices. Feeling judged can impact self-esteem and confidence.

Experiencing judgment can impact us in deeply personal ways:

> Judging someone can have similar effects to other forms of discrimination. People describe feeling isolated, ashamed, misunderstood, criticized and demeaned. Judging can also result in people being less likely to talk about what they're going through and ask for the help they need.[10]

## How judgment serves us

Judgment serves us brilliantly as a survival tool, allowing us to quickly and efficiently assess situations, events and people. When we judge others, we protect ourselves and identify opportunities. Maybe you see the best in someone whom others overlook. Perhaps your judgment empowers you to consider someone's potential contribution to the company, whereas your peers only consider past experience or educational pedigree as an indicator of success. Maybe you rely on "gut" to form opinions, while your colleagues look for data. Judgment impacts perception and is the key driver we look to affect when it comes to rebuilding and repairing reputation after damage or crisis. More on this in Chapter 6.

## Belief

When we tell someone "I believe in you... or God... or the power of positive thinking... or not eating after 9 pm," we are saying that we have formed an opinion so strong and powerful to us that we place trust and confidence in that belief, and we will defend the position during contrary opinion or challenge.

Beliefs can be faith-based, culturally based, experience-based or evidence-based. They are often rooted in moral codes and values statements. Once someone declares a thing as a "belief," we suppose it has moved through being a suspicion, idea or feeling to being more trusted and certain in the mind (and heart) of the believer.

Beliefs cause us to take a leap of faith or to act, regardless of evidence:

- I believe if I invest in this stock, based on the recommendations I read from Joe Smith, I'll make money.
- I believe if I follow this leader, I'll be "chosen" by God.
- I believe if I eat these supplements, I'll lose weight.
- I believe if I take care of my people, they'll work hard for me.

When beliefs are shattered, as can happen if the belief system was not founded on something qualified, the person who held that belief dearly can feel devastated. When you invest based on beliefs about the investment guru, and ultimately lose money... When you end up in the hospital because the diet supplements made you ill... When you invest in a servant leadership model only to have your workers betray you... it can shatter your belief system and ability to trust. Imagine you believed your parent when they said they would stop drinking, and therefore would stop hurting you and your brother. You have no evidence to see they will change, but you desperately want them to. When they don't change the behavior, and you are hurt again, you begin to question everything an adult tells you.

## Beliefs should be challenged

With perception and reputation, beliefs are critical. Throughout this book we will challenge your beliefs about what is, and isn't, what we know versus what we believe to be true. Separating fact from belief is helpful in managing how and where we can make impact, who we can influence, and why we seek to inspire others. What can happen when you challenge beliefs is that you feel a need to dig in deeper to support your confirmation bias and beliefs: "I insist that is true and real. It is a belief I have had my whole life!" This resistance is normal, but so is the opportunity to look into the structure of the belief to see if there are flaws or ways to modify its foundation, and therefore create a better structure.

Consider this example: For as long as he could remember, Mike wanted to run a company. At the age of seven, he opened a lemonade stand and pocketed $36 in his first month. Quite a windfall for a young child! After numerous paper routes, pizza delivery jobs and lawn mowing businesses during high school, Mike entered college to study business and entrepreneurship. Mike believed that being your own boss meant complete financial, personal and spiritual independence. "No one can tell me what to do if I'm the boss," he once told me. "And that's how I like it, just me." Complete independence, to Mike, was as vital as air is to you and me.

But later, after his third startup imploded due to lack of sound business planning, Mike found himself courting investors and strategic business partners for the first time. The process of bringing others in to have a stake in his companies, and a say in how they were run, threatened his independence. He stressed over every percentage of equity he had to part with in exchange for investment. He bristled at every alternative opinion shared on his business practices. He panicked each time one of his business partners said they wanted to "sit with him and talk," fearing he'd have to give up more and more of what he held most dear—his independence.

Together, we reframed his belief about independence, pulling out the assets from the belief that worked for Mike, and shelving the ones that only served to promote fear and anger. Separating the fact from emotion was key for Mike to look at the bigger picture of his situation: With these investors and strategic business partners working alongside him offering input, resources and guidance, and yes, taking equity and attention from Mike, he was actually gaining more independence than when he held all the responsibilities close to him and worked nights and weekends to keep it all moving. Giving some control away actually gave Mike more independence. This new belief and thinking rewired his approach to business and led him to scale quicker than he ever imagined.

## Trust

What greater attribute is there than trust? We live in a world of skepticism, of wanting to kick the tires before we buy. Consumers are taught to read reviews, talk to their neighbors and purchase with reservation. Yet, leaders whip up crowds by declaring, "You can trust me!" Years ago, I authored an article about trust titled, "Saying you're a good kisser doesn't make it true." While the title got a lot of attention, the message was that you simply can't mandate someone to trust you. Trust is earned. Just like being a good kisser, it's really up to others to determine that attribute to you, not for you to proclaim yourself. Only other people can call you trustworthy; it's not enough to say it about yourself.

In reputation management, trust is vital. If a professional or entrepreneur or business leader or contributor is seen as trustworthy, we give them latitude when they blunder, we forgive their missteps, and we bring them closer into confidential conversations. If someone is seen as inauthentic, leery or untrustworthy, it's extremely hard to build rapport with a target audience and then move through a process ending in relationship. Susan, a client I worked with, stated it this way: "No matter how many degrees you have, what fancy schools you attended, or the years you've been in business, if I don't get the sense I can trust you, I won't hire you." Pedigree and experience don't trump rapport, ease and trust.

*How does trust influence perception?*

Each year since 2000, the global communications firm Edelman publishes its annual Trust Barometer. For business leaders, public relations professionals, entrepreneurs and industry followers, this report is invaluable as an indicator of the relationship between consumer and business. Where there is trust, business thrives. Where there is fracture, business suffers.

In its 2020 Trust Barometer, Edelman points to growing fractures in trust-building, loyalty and the ability to leverage trust beyond the company (to its leaders):

> A majority of respondents in every developed market do not believe
> they will be better off in five years' time, and more than half of
> respondents globally believe that capitalism in its current form is now
> doing more harm than good in the world.
>
> The result is a world of two different trust realities. The informed
> public—wealthier, more educated, and frequent consumers of news—
> remain far more trusting of every institution than the mass population.
> In a majority of markets, less than half of the mass population trust
> their institutions to do what is right. There are now a record eight
> markets showing all-time-high gaps between the two audiences—an
> alarming trust inequality.[11]

This finding is particularly noteworthy because business leaders, influencers and entrepreneurs today are pushed to be trustworthy, to showcase their vulnerability, offer up their needs and connect with audiences more genuinely than ever before to build trust. As they build trust, the company thrives. If markets no longer trust the companies, they may now distrust the leaders of those companies. This is often driven all by perception.

*What happens when trust is broken*

In any relationship—marriage, business investment, employment arrangement—when trust is broken, the relationship is at risk of complete failure. When the CEO tells employees that "Everything will be okay, we'll just find a new partner" after a major supplier goes bankrupt, those employees trust they mean what they say. When no replacement purveyor is found, the company fails to meet deliveries and is forced to lay off staff, remaining employees may believe the CEO lied and misled them, ignoring the fact they tried and failed to keep things moving forward. Remaining employees might begin looking for other jobs, discount the CEO's future messages, and might even distrust all management at the company. Trust is sacred, and when broken, fear and greed step in to take over.

## In closing

Numerous articles and research studies point out that perception drives belief and belief drives behavior. To understand how you'll build and promote an intentional and authentic personal brand, it's important to understand that judgment, trust, optics and other influences color the ultimate impression you'll make. In conversation, we often use the terms interchangeably—perception, impression, judgment, belief—but as we've seen here, they mean different things. We are navigating judgments and beliefs people have about us and people like us. Those judgments can show up as stereotypes and biases, limiting the opportunities we can pursue or affording us more opportunities because of the perception in favor of who we are or what we represent.

Our ultimate goal is to be able to live authentically, meaningfully and completely, to build relationships with people we seek to inspire, influence and impact, and to be rewarded for our effort. To do so, we must understand the belief systems and values of those individuals, navigate biases and perceptions, and drive an impression that positively affects our position.

# Endnotes

**1**  Berns, G (2010) *Iconoclast*, Harvard Business Review Press, Boston

**2**  Diversity.ucsf.edu (2020) Unconscious bias, Diversity.ucsf.edu, https://diversity.ucsf.edu/resources/unconscious-bias (archived at https://perma.cc/62EW-6VNN)

**3**  Neuroscience News (2020) Analyzing the complexity of our perception, *Neuroscience News*, https://neurosciencenews.com/perception-objects-recognition-3704/ (archived at https://perma.cc/M2D9-8FES)

**4**  Ibid

**5**  Isabella, G, Mazzon, J A and Dimoka, A (2015) Culture differences, difficulties, and challenges of the neurophysiological methods in marketing research, https://www.tandfonline.com/doi/abs/10.1080/08961530.2015.1038761 (archived at https://perma.cc/7AY8-F3EF)

**6**  Balboa, N and Glaser, R D (2020) The neuroscience of identity, The CreatingWE® Institute, https://creatingwe.com/news-blogs/articles-blogs/psychology-today/the-neuroscience-of-identity (archived at https://perma.cc/R5Z7-M9PS)

**7**  Psychology (2020) Moral judgment, Iresearchnet, http://psychology.iresearchnet.com/sports-psychology/moral-development/moral-judgment/ (archived at https://perma.cc/89P4-MLQ6)

**8**  Social Psych Online (2016) Psychology of judging people: 3 ways we judge others, Social Psych Online, http://socialpsychonline.com/2016/10/judging-people-psychology/ (archived at https://perma.cc/X4LU-6U7F)

**9**  Quoteinvestigator.com (2014) You'll worry less about what people think about you when you realize how seldom they do, https://quoteinvestigator.com/2014/09/09/worry-less (archived at https://perma.cc/JF9L-W2D3)

**10**  Time to Change (2020) The impact of judgement, https://www.time-to-change.org.uk/about-us/our-campaigns/challenging-stigma-young-people/impact-judgement (archived at https://perma.cc/3D8L-UPE2)

**11**  Edelman (2020) 2020 Edelman Trust Barometer, https://www.edelman.com/trustbarometer (archived at https://perma.cc/8TFH-EJFK)

# 02

# Changing perception through personal branding

*How does personal branding work to affect, manipulate and manage reputation and perception? Here, we'll examine case studies and examples to see how changing perception works using personal branding systems.*

Imagine you are in need of an accountant for your investment firm. You want to hire someone with large-firm experience, who's skilled at managing the financial details of multiple portfolio companies and complex ownership structures. You also want them to help you pay the least taxes possible without going to jail. You interview two final accountant prospects. The first one, Bob, grew his career in one of the Big Four accounting firms, has deep experience with complex tax structures and touts an Ivy League education. The second one, Jim, is also knowledgeable on tax structures for firms like yours, grew his career working with his father's boutique firm, received his education from a state college before passing the CPA exam and comes highly recommended from your personal attorney. On paper, both candidates are technically qualified to handle your business accounting needs.

When you interview them, Bob talks about his qualifications, his schooling, his impressive client list and his notable track record. Jim, on the other hand, asks you questions about your business goals, why you started the firm, how you select companies to invest in, and what you dream about. Both are qualified, but Jim feels like he cares about you and your business. You hire Jim because he feels like a partner, not a vendor.

Personal branding takes into account that all things considered equal—both are qualified—you will choose to work with someone you feel a connection with, a synergy. Or, if you don't feel a compelling reason to choose one, you may simply choose one in order to not choose the other. If Bob comes off as arrogant and stubborn, you might choose Jim simply to avoid working with Bob.

Widespread belief among marketing practitioners promotes that we *act on logic* (I need an accountant) but we *buy on emotion* (Jim gets me!). Here, we will take a deeper look at how personal branding works, why it's critical in twenty-first-century business, entrepreneurship and thought leadership, and what happens when a strong, consistent and compelling personal brand is missing.

## Personal branding explained

In 1997, Tom Peters authored an article for *Fast Company* that changed the way we saw ourselves and our careers. In the piece, Peters proclaimed:

> Regardless of age, regardless of position, regardless of the business we happen to be in, all of us need to understand the importance of branding. We are CEOs of our own companies: Me Inc. To be in business today, our most important job is to be head marketer for the brand called You.[1]

Peters was describing a new career ecosystem, an intricate web of intentional and strategic tools we can develop for ourselves that gives us positioning, recognition, referability and credibility. Instead of leaving our fate (and reputation) up to those people around us, we were now encouraged to be proactive and take control over how we are perceived. The concept of personal branding was, by most accounts, born. Personal branding today involves the use of digital platforms and tools to help us position and promote ourselves. When

Peters emphasized personal branding, he focused on several of the same systems, and his teachings gave us enough of a base to add social media, social networking and online reputation management opportunities (and challenges) to the mix.

Personal branding is the way you position yourself: the web of interlaced impressions that drive an intentional perception with your target audience. Personal branding, when done correctly, offers you an organizing set of principles through which to make all decisions— how you'll show up, form relationships, carry yourself and build an intentional legacy. Personal branding is about perception, identity and ultimately legacy: Who are you, what do you care about, and how do you want others to feel about you? Judith Glaser, mentioned previously, offers this explanation:

> Three main constituents of identity are how you view yourself, how others view you, and how you judge/act based on others' perceptions of you. Whether or not the perspectives are those of your immediate friends, family, or the social norms of your culture, they significantly shape your sense of identity.[2]

Our sense of identity—who we are, what we value, what we offer— directly influences and drives our personal brand strategy and anchors in values and goals. Through the process of building a brand, you uncover marketable assets, character traits and qualities, as well as the blind spots you need to correct. It is a process of self-discovery and goal-setting, focused on specific audiences and objectives.

## Who needs to worry about building a brand?

Once, during the questions and answers portion of a large lecture I delivered, a participant in the back of the room asked, "If I want to continue working as a doctor, I don't need to focus on this branding stuff, right?" His theory was that if a patient needs a doctor, they hire a doctor. In other words, as a doctor, he didn't need to concern himself with positioning himself. Was he right? His belief was that his patients needed to engage with him, therefore positioning really was irrelevant: As long as he could perform the medical procedures patients needed, he was set. My response to him was, "If you interact with other people, you need to build and maintain a strong personal brand. I guess the only job where it wouldn't matter might be if you work as a hitman."

College students, financial executives, doctors, authors, business leaders, entrepreneurs, cartoonists, project managers, physicists, beauty pageant contestants, real estate developers, tech giants, professional athletes, software developers, scientists, researchers, teachers, non-profit leaders, social justice advocates, venture capitalists: I've worked with them all. Each one approached the personal branding and reputation management process with a similar question, "Does someone like me need to be concerned with what other people think about me?" Yes.

I've worked with young adults who've been entrepreneurs since they could remember but feared investors wouldn't take them seriously. I've worked with senior executives who worried that their life was coming to a close and they didn't have much time left to leave the legacy they desired. I've coached mothers returning to the workforce after an absence of many years, and professional athletes who feared they couldn't find a purpose after sports. For each of them, and perhaps for you, the idea of taking control over the way they are perceived is both intriguing and terrifying at the same time.

I remember working with Mary, a leader in the field of addiction recovery who'd authored several books, led workshops of thousands of people and called the first-class section of American Airlines "home." Mary had built a huge following of recovering addicts, families living with addiction, therapists and medical practitioners who hung onto her methodology, research and approach to care for struggling patients. When I first met Mary, one of her first comments to me was:

> I'm 70 years young. I know there isn't as much runway in front of me as behind, but I want to be sure my legacy accurately reflects who I am and why I cared about my work. Not just the impact or process of my work.

Mary wanted to be in control over how her story was told, even after she was no longer involved in telling it. This is a common concern for many professionals, regardless of their age or experience.

If you work in a field where you don't want to be found or are the only person in the entire universe who does a particular service or has a specific skill that no one else has, then maybe you can disregard the way people feel about you and how you're perceived. For the rest of us, we know we are competing with others who are equally talented, qualified and experienced who offer similar work, product, service and expertise. Our ability to stand apart, differentiate our value and create an experience with our target audience is critical in the twenty-first-century global economy.

## What happens without a personal brand strategy?

Most professionals don't think about their personal brand as they spring from college, university or graduate school into their careers. They focus on gathering career experience, building networks of valuable contacts, accumulating knowledge and skills to make them more valuable to the next employer/client/investor. These professionals likely were encouraged by parents, business school professors and career advisors to stay open and neutral to opportunities so as not to "close any doors" that could limit them later. Good advice, sort of. At the same time, we are being reassured by our parents, coaches, mentors and advisors that "it doesn't matter what other people think about you. It just matters what you believe about yourself—what's in your heart." And they are half-right. Now, we know that it does matter what other people think about us because how they perceive us directly impacts and influences whether they want to offer us opportunities, advance us in our careers, and refer us to others. So, while it does matter what's in our heart… it also matters how other people perceive us.

*When the marketplace defines you*

Without a strategic and intentional personal brand strategy, the market defines you. Competition for opportunities becomes fierce, and your relevance and reputation can be misunderstood, overlooked or negative. This is the case for many professionals today who find themselves passed up or dismissed for key opportunities. Many factors impact how the market will define you. Which market are you competing in? If you care mostly about how your peers, colleagues, staff and executive team perceive you, that may be your "market." If you are more focused on public perception, media attention and customer input, the aperture of your defined market opens more widely.

Regardless of who you determine is your market, recognize that they will form a perception of you, either on their own or with your input and direction. As we saw in Chapter 1, perception is highly influenced by the emotional, cultural and environmental filters someone brings into their understanding, but as the title of this book notes, you can "control the narrative" and drive perception. In most cases, the reason the market defines someone is simply because no focus, attention or effort was put towards managing and directing their perception. Simply assuming that people will "get" you, find you valuable and compelling and want to hire you is naïve. There is so much information made available through the internet and social media that if you aren't driving the narrative, you are giving up authorship of your own story.

*Risks of letting the market define you*

When you leave to chance that others will find you relevant, compelling, interesting and valuable, you give away a lot of your power and control. Aside from emotional filters and biases, your target audience could compare you to others who are less qualified or be misinformed about who you are and what you stand for. For example, when I began working in reputation management and personal branding, few people understood the term "personal branding." Even my executive clients would call what I did "executive coaching," "impression management" or "image consulting" because they were unclear about what it meant to build a personal brand. In managing and directing my own brand, I needed to clearly, confidently and consistently promote my skills under the heading of personal branding, and I was burdened with defining what it meant, which problems I solved, and why potential clients needed to hire me. And, I needed to differentiate myself from others who might eventually use the same term ("personal branding") but mean a different service and experience. Over time, the values I stood for, the brand I built and the understanding of what I do became clearer and I found the narrative more easily controlled.

When we leave our reputation up to the imagination of others, we forfeit the opportunity to explain how we are uniquely valuable to them. We risk being seen as generic or being grouped with others who've chartered unique (and very different) brands from us.

Consider the following examples:

- Fred, a financial planner, is often asked, "Oh, so you're like a Suze Orman?"

- Jennifer, who's passionate about international travel and adventure, is told, "I know what you do—I've got a cousin who likes to escape real life, too."

- Chris, an Army veteran, is asked, "So, you have anger issues? I mean, isn't that why people join the military?"

*The market can define you positively, though*

Even if you have let the market define you and have not been strategic about shaping others' perception of you, it doesn't mean the public perception of you will automatically be negative. When Greg, a leading executive in the employee benefits field, hired me, he was looking to understand why he was so popular with his clients. He said:

> I have a great client base of wonderful, long-term accounts. My clients tell me how much they value my services; they are loyal and refer other

companies to work with me often. The challenge is that I don't know what I did to earn such praise and loyalty.

He continued, "I want to retire in ten years. My fear is that if I'm not clear on what I did to get *here*, I might mess it up and lose the credibility, reputation and business I've earned." In his case, nothing was wrong—Greg just wanted to understand what levers were available to him so he could ensure a similar track record for the remainder of his career.

In working with Greg, we spent a lot of time in the assessment phase, doing an inventory of his brand. We assessed his values, goals, behavior and communications styles. We looked back over wins and losses, opportunities and challenges, and how he'd navigated them. Then, we examined his client relationships. After conducting email and phone interviews with his long-term clients, we were able to identify key patterns:

- Greg's clients never felt "sold to." They truly believed that when Greg offered a new product or service, or their premiums changed, it was in the client's best interest to do so. Greg had established tremendous credibility with his clients through his consistent transparency of communication—several clients even spoke of times Greg showed them how to push back on a rate increase to get more favorable terms, or when he explained that a fancy new product would not serve the client long term.

- Greg was highly trusted by his clients. They described him as part of their company's family. This was a behavior Greg never realized he was exhibiting, but when we discussed it, he thoroughly agreed with them—"I've been to their kids' weddings and baptisms," he proudly proclaimed. "In some cases, our wives even get together to socialize."

- His humor and playfulness were seen as refreshing. A few of Greg's clients offered feedback on their service provider prior to Greg: "Business had always been so serious. When we met Greg, it was still a serious business, but he made it fun. He helped us enjoy the process."

- Finally, the most notable feedback on Greg's brand came from a client who described him this way: "I feel like Greg lives and breathes employee benefits. I truly believe he thinks about our company's needs as he's drifting off to sleep at night. That makes me feel very safe working with Greg. He makes us feel safe."

Words that emerged from this research into Greg's work style and personal brand included: transparent, trust, credibility, social/personable/approachable, fun and safe. To Greg, this aligned perfectly with how he wanted to be known. Having clear and explicit examples of how his desired reputation was showing up for his clients on a daily basis empowered us to create a thoughtful and intentional strategy to make sure Greg continued to do what he was doing, which was clearly working for him!

The plan I built and coached Greg towards included several strategies to capitalize on the keywords that he wanted to pursue, and which his existing clients already said mattered to them (and earned their loyalty). Going forward, Greg was more mindful of using the specific words that would resonate with his clients and attract new clients, and he felt more in control of how the remaining ten years of his career would play out.

## Brands are driven by feelings

A personal brand is that quality that you assign words to, and you just *feel* about someone... that *je ne sais quoi* that makes one person more interesting, relevant, valuable and worth pursuing. It's sometimes hard to pinpoint where it starts, but you just know when it's there and you may even question how your feelings towards that person developed. Does that mean personal branding is about altering or affecting perception? Yes.

Brands make us feel something—they make us feel confident, powerful, safe or proud. Or brands can make us feel unworthy, inadequate, fearful or shamed. In product branding, the focus is always on the *expectation of the experience* the target consumer will have of that product: What do we want them to feel when they hold our razor? What beliefs will they have about their life if they buy this computer? How will that customer feel about themselves when they drive away in our car? To illustrate, imagine if I were to go test drive a high-end luxury sports car. I have certain beliefs around what that experience would be like. I believe I'll get behind the steering wheel of the beautifully crafted automobile, sink comfortably into the finely engineered leather seats and when the engine turns over and begins to roar... I'll feel invincible, confident, sexy and successful. I expect that when I drive down the street in this fancy car, people will look at me and wonder, "Who is that beautiful, successful and powerful woman (who can afford such a special car)?" They will watch (with envy) as I speed past them in this amazing machine. This is my perception of the expectation of the experience I'd have driving this car. And, if that experience is valuable and attractive enough to me, I will find a way to afford such a luxury to have that feeling more often.

Because brands are based on feelings and expectations (beliefs and perception), much of the conversation around personal brand-building and repair focuses on emotion. To reiterate, while there are many behaviors and feelings that drive buying behavior, it is that long-held belief by marketing practitioners that buyers act on logic (I need a new car) and buy on emotion (THIS car makes me feel confident, influential, accomplished). Brand attributes in product marketing are critical to sales success. Even outside of product marketing, we know that feelings are critical to effecting change and influencing others. Feelings drive the power we have to control the narrative and in personal branding they are the foundation for the experience we'll have for the people we want to attract to us.

## How a personal brand impacts how you're perceived

If you were being introduced to a potential board member, and another board member warned you that this candidate was known for being ruthless, aggressive and indiscreet, how do you think that first meeting would go? You'd likely meet them with skepticism and would be reluctant to impart confidential company information for fear they'd share it. Similarly, if you knew nothing about this potential board member, but you researched them online and saw photos of them partying with young girls in tropical settings, would you think they exercised poor judgment?

Reputation built on word of mouth and online information tells only part of the story. It is limited to the viewpoint of the person sharing the insight (in this case, your current board member) or specific information channels online. While we know this is not a complete picture of who the person is, what they stand for and how they can add value, we begin to form a perception about them without even realizing it. One of the hardest skills I had to learn in working with clients was to not form a perception about a client prior to working with them. Yes, I have to interview them, and they interview me. We evaluate each other and whether we're a fit to accomplish specific goals. I conduct online research to uncover hidden traps in their reputation I might encounter as I advise them. But my job is to keep an open mind as I help them navigate their reputational challenges and opportunities.

It might seem simple: Just refrain from forming an opinion or judgment. But, as we saw in Chapter 1, judgment, beliefs and perception are habitual. "Keeping an open mind" is sometimes easier said than done. One technique I use to manage my own perception of prospective clients and their situations is to remember to focus on what is most consistent, not what is unusual. *Personal branding is all about consistency—when more often I see you acting or speaking or behaving a certain way, I'll believe it.* Every once in a while, we all make mistakes, fall off script and deviate from our brand path. Those should be seen as the exceptions. We can trust that which is most consistent with what we expect and believe to be true about the person when there is enough consistent evidence to show who they truly are.

### Perception can work against you

In working with a new client, I'll often examine multiple sites to see what I can learn about them. Instead of just reading the leading news headlines, I'll look for any assets the client manages for themselves, such as social media channels. I'll read their recommendations on LinkedIn, peruse their Facebook profile, read what former employees say about them on Glassdoor and so on. While it's tempting to believe the headlines are all true, often there is more to the story.

Still refraining from forming judgment (as best I can), I'll assess how the person is positioned, positively or negatively, and what actions they might have taken to manage or influence that perception. If the information online is all negative, for instance, and the individual has no proactive counter-positioning efforts anywhere, that tells one story. If they've lashed out in the comments section of news articles, posted blogs and videos professing their innocence, that tells another story. Often, when negative information appears about someone online, other online users jump into the mix. Trolls, angry former employees, disgruntled workers, irritated journalists and general naysayers may offer up their views and opinions using the anonymous cloak of the internet. Similarly, employees, peers and other advocates could rally to support the individual and that's also worth noting.

Perception, over time, does start to feel real. For the client who's tried to show who they are and failed to build rapport with their target audience, it can be extremely frustrating. Online readers can begin to believe what they read and feel that if there was another story to be told, surely the individual would have done so. If only it were that easy.

### Perception can work in your favor

The positive side of personal branding is that the transfer of credibility, trust and perception can also work to serve you. When people believe positive traits, qualities and values assigned to you, they will tell others. If those qualities are consistent with what you desire, and you act reliably with how they believe you to be, your ability to be referred and endorsed grows exponentially. For most of us, referrals and word-of-mouth marketing are the most cost-effective ways to expand our business, influence and reach. Online and in person, when someone else touts our value and others take notice, our business significance and importance rise. For years, professionals and other online users held onto the score they received through a now-defunct website and its unique algorithm called "klout." This "score" claimed to indicate someone's level of relevance. Even today, clout (defined as influence or power, for instance in politics or business) is still used to refer to someone's importance, recognition and brand influence.

Brand influence matters because if you're unknown or unrecognized for your ability to contribute, you risk being passed up. When we say we care about reach and authority, we mean we care that we are seen as compelling and relevant by the audience we seek to influence, inspire and impact. When we are seen positively, recognized for our contribution and offer, and are highly referred and endorsed, the threshold for consideration by others is lowered. Ideal prospects and opportunities flood towards us as if by magic. We are attracting exactly what we seek, and the effort seems almost minimal. But it's not. Personal branding sets the stage for this magic. By crafting and deploying a strategic brand program, living authentically and consistently through personal values, and earning the trust and credibility of a target audience, you reap the rewards of success. Branding is the hard part; living that brand is often much easier.

### Perception can reveal opportunity

Being able to inventory and evaluate the perception that exists in the market about you can reveal tremendous opportunity and insight. Here's an example of how this works: When I launched my company in 2008, I'd left a long-standing career in corporate branding and marketing, having worked for some remarkable and impactful global brands across many industries. As I launched LIDA360 in 2008, I knew I needed to inventory my reputation so I could evaluate the assets (or detractors) I was working with and which I'd need to build off of or repair. What I discovered surprised and humbled me. Up to that point I'd spent my career focused on getting to whatever was next: driving, growing, accelerating growth at all turns. While I enjoyed many years of personal and professional "success," I'd held my foot firmly on the gas pedal of my career, projects, teams and the groups I led. To say I was always moving fast would be an understatement. This was reflected in the feedback I gathered about my brand and reputation as I set out to build my company.

In 2008, I would have described myself as "determined, competitive, and focused on excellence," yet I received candid feedback from trusted advisors who offered up words like "cutthroat", "aggressive" and "non-collaborative." Oops! This was not the brand I wanted to portray in my next venture. After swallowing hard and taking a pause, I realized the opportunity to learn from this perception feedback. While it certainly stung to hear these insights, I quickly saw that I'd received valuable insight into my blind spots. Had I not received this input I would have possibly pursued opportunities with a style that was off-putting and could have hurt relationships I valued. Instead, I learned where I could pivot, how I could capitalize on my strengths and where I could work through my weaknesses. In personal branding, the goal is consistency and not perfection, remember, but I needed to make significant adjustments to my attitude, behavior, interactions and communication so that my truest value came forward and wasn't overshadowed by my demeanor or delivery.

We'll discuss the concept of feedback, pivoting and modifying your behavior to get results throughout this book, as they are key aspects to building a sustainable and scalable personal brand. Without the ability to flex and adjust, we run the risk of becoming obsolete or getting too deeply rooted in a system or reputation such that we can't grow, personally and professionally. Perception, while very personal, can give us the insight we need to adjust in meaningful and authentic ways.

## Trust and credibility drive brands

Another theme you'll hear throughout this book is the importance of trust and credibility. For most of my work, I avoid industries where trust is not manageable, or could be constructed in artificial ways. We know that it's possible to put "spin" on a story, or to Photoshop an image to create a false impression. Those tactics, while still prevalent in some industries and professions, are not authentic or sustainable. Instead, when executives, entrepreneurs, leaders and professionals strive for trust and credibility, they find more opportunity to be genuine in their relationships, candid in their expression of their values and they attract like-minded individuals. The opportunities they also attract feel more consistent and "on brand" and career acceleration seems easier.

Personal branding is all about trust. Your brand will be grounded in a common and clearly articulated set of values and passions which others can rely upon, and on which you can be trusted to live and act. When someone has established a strong and consistent brand, and we see them suddenly act "out of character," we attribute it to an off day and not a fracture in brand. If there are no clearly established credibility and trust in place, every misstep or misbehavior is attributed to who we believe that person is and not to a mistake. Just as Edelman looks at trust with global business brands, we can assess and test our trustability and credibility with the audiences we seek to build relationships with. One easy way to see this is by actually asking—do you trust me? Do you trust that I'll represent you and your goals? Do you believe me when I tell you I'm passionate about solving this problem? Do you see me as a credible resource for...?

## Values and actions drive beliefs

Similarly, our values and actions reinforce perception by driving others to see—and believe—who we are and what we hold dear. People are looking for evidence of your values and consistency in your actions to live them. If you tell me you're passionate about social justice causes, yet I see no evidence of this (online or in your actions), I'll question it. Often, someone will profess allegiance to a cause or concern, yet there is nothing in their history or current behavior that supports their commitment. They simply want to join the bandwagon of a trending initiative or idea. This is also where brands can fracture.

We seek proof and evidence through actions, but most target audiences aren't expecting heroic or extreme displays of this commitment. If you say you stand behind your employees' actions, we expect to see you back them up when there's a problem. If you pledge to return exponential value to shareholders, we assume you'll make fiscally sound decisions which support their investment in you and the business. In many cases, I'd advise a client to *not* issue a public proclamation unless they thoroughly understand how the narrative plays out: Are you truly willing and ready to pivot what might need to change so you can back up this assertion? How long can you stay committed to this direction?

Early on, an environmental entrepreneur client of mine was given a prime opportunity to present at a major conference of other entrepreneurs, media and investors. He knew the event had a more "conservative" slant to it, and the investors attending came from more traditional investment banking careers and institutions. This particular client was all about pushing boundaries, independent thinking, innovation and disruption. He'd have to now cater to an audience that valued a more traditional approach for their portfolio companies. In discussing the opportunity with him, we evaluated the short-term and long-term benefits of the opportunity. For example, at such an event he could certainly attract new investors, but would he want those investors? What would that experience be like for him and the company? He would certainly attract new entrepreneur friends, colleagues and possible strategic partnerships. But would they see him the same way once he was back home, in his office, working with his natural disruptor nature? We evaluated whether he'd be able to successfully communicate his vision—and the vision of his company—authentically and with the same vigor and intensity he would if he was in a room of like-minded individuals, similarly passionate about solving the same issues, in a similar way. Or, would catering to this audience cause him to appear disingenuous or even dishonest?

Finally, we discussed the long-term brand implications to him and his business if either path proved true: he was able to build relationship with audiences he didn't like or feel authentic around, or if later they saw him as dishonest. The event wasn't a make-or-break business opportunity, but it was an interesting exercise to run through how he could show up and what the implications and perception could be that would reflect back on him and his business.

In evaluating opportunities, remember that your values play an important role in not only your personal brand development but also how you deploy and live that brand. When your actions align with your values, you build credibility and people can trust you. Without action, values are hollow, they appear to be "lip service." Without values tied to them, your actions can be misinterpreted and misunderstood by your audiences.

## Corporate versus personal brands: Don't confuse them

Today, many professionals find the line between their personal and company brands blurred. The CEO of a popular company is often noted as the "face of the brand," even unwittingly. Team members for a brand might find their personal values and beliefs spilling into public forums online, confusing customers if their view conflicts with the company brand. As more and more people post on social media, engage in public discourse and form external relationships, they are also becoming the brand of the company.

Years ago, I worked with a young and brilliant CEO of a technology startup. This company was on the verge of tremendous success, gaining the attention of many investment suitors, channel partners, media and others as their technology solved an important global problem. The immediate issue, however, was that the CEO's personal brand didn't align with the company positioning. The CEO, Hector, had grown up in the tech world as a classic tech startup story: He developed unique and innovative systems in his garage, got his start as an early employee of some (now) tech giants, and could quickly scare anyone not techie with his theories around cyber threats and data mining leaks. It was Hector's track record, knowledge and his over-the-top boisterous personality that often gained him notice. A conversation with Hector was always exciting and terrifying all at the same time. He delivered stories and theories as Academy Award-worthy performances!

Hector's personality was "large and in charge," as he liked to profess. He commanded the room with his deep voice and outlandish style. Never one to dress "corporate" or follow professional protocols, he relished his style as an outlier: a technology superstar with a larger-than-life personality. While his employees, friends, professional colleagues and followers loved his eccentric style, his investors didn't. They tolerated his personality to a point. When it came time to pursue additional rounds of funding and participate in important road shows with potential investors, the feedback cited concerns about his executive presence, his ability to stay focused on growing the business, and his capacity to maintain relationships with key accounts over time without losing interest. If we didn't redirect Hector's positioning, and posture the company brand as unique from him, the risk was high that they wouldn't eventually get to IPO stage or even sale.

For several months we worked on developing Hector's brand online and in person. We started with adjusting his image and key strategic relationships. He went on a personal brand tour visiting clients, investors and important channel partners within key sectors. He polished his style a bit, toned down his flair for the dramatic, and tailored his approach to each conversation. He was not changing who he was or being disingenuous. Rather, he amended and modified his style to be appropriate to the situation. For an investor meeting, he was well briefed on financial forecasts, pricing models and growth forecasts for the company. For meetings with influencers and referral sources, he paid more attention to helping them see the benefit of working with him to their own business and customer base. He became skilled at speaking to the needs of the people he was serving.

Later, when the time came for him to sell the company, he'd successfully separated his unique personality from the organization and it was easier for acquirers to see how they could buy the company, incorporate the technology into their own portfolio, and Hector could remain involved as an asset. Taking the spotlight off himself allowed Hector to create a viable company for acquisition and growth.

Here's another example of how this works: I was referred to Martin by a member of his board of directors. They were beginning his transition from CEO into retirement, and the board was concerned that Martin's name (and reputation) was so closely intertwined with the company that separating the two could be problematic upon his departure. Martin had founded the early childhood education company 25 years prior and was ready to do something new. He'd become a well-recognized speaker, author—with 14 books to his credit—and lecturer on unique approaches to personalized learning for children. His work garnered him regular media attention and he was seen as an expert in his field, an expert who was the CEO of a growing company with which his name was synonymous.

Martin wasn't planning to slow down and play golf in retirement. He wanted to continue writing and speaking on similar topics to those he'd covered before, but he needed to separate from the legacy brand he'd built through his company. How could we disconnect his name from the company so he could do something else and the company could continue to thrive in his absence (he would remain as a board member but have a limited role after retirement)? Our strategy began with the transition narrative: Why was Martin leaving the company as CEO, where was he headed, why was the change timely and important to the company's trajectory? With a media tour and targeted customer promotions, we controlled the story around the change and stopped any speculation about his departure before it started. We brought the new CEO into the conversation as well, to showcase continuity of passion and experience.

The board and new CEO played an active role in this announcement rollout. They were interviewed alongside Martin, starred in a transition video we created to run at major events, on social media and the website, and the new CEO slowly began to field inquiries and take the more prominent role as the face of the organization. While this approach might seem routine for a high-profile C-level transition, in Martin's case, his visibility tied to the company was extraordinary. We needed to show that the institutional knowledge he'd baked into the fibers of the company would still be there, even if he was gone from day-to-day operations. This part was tricky. As we continued the migration over to the new CEO, there remained times when journalists or investors still insisted on speaking instead to Martin about developments. The 18 months prior to his exit were spent navigating (with finesse) these conversations.

But Martin was still concerned about his personal brand and reputation after he departed. Would he be viable and interesting to his community once his title changed? For his own branding and reputation needs, we decided he would take a short sabbatical prior to officially exiting as CEO. This was an untraditional move, given the company was in the midst of a leadership transition. We used the three months of his sabbatical to set Martin up for new positioning— he registered a new LLC under his own name, authored several "letters to the editor" and articles for leading journals and publications, talked about his vision for his future and contribution to the field, and held many strategic networking lunches and dinners with key influencers who were now meeting Martin, the consultant, instead of Martin, the CEO of his legacy company.

In the end, the transition was smooth, and Martin was able to swiftly move from CEO to transitioning CEO to sabbatical to consultant/business owner, with his own brand. The company was poised to thrive and continue its mission to serve the greater mission of helping children learn.

## In closing

Who needs personal branding? We all do. Wherever you are in life, whatever station you're in as you read this, your personal brand is how you communicate your value to the audiences who must find and understand you. Without a strong and intentional brand, you risk being misunderstood, overlooked or deemed irrelevant. With a personal brand, you are leveraging the power of influence and narrative to direct your audience towards the perception you seek them to have of you.

Personal branding is not about "spin" or reinvention or distracting your target audience such that they see something inauthentic as real. Personal branding is rooted in trust and credibility and must be led through your values and passions. Then, when you tell yourself you're worthy and why you're valuable, and others begin to appreciate and refer you for that value, opportunities appear!

## Endnotes

1  Peters, T (1997) The brand called you, *Fast Company*, https://www.fastcompany.com/28905/brand-called-you (archived at https://perma.cc/4AVE-6EEH)
2  Balboa, N and Glaser, R (2019) The neuroscience of identity, *Psychology Today*, https://www.psychologytoday.com/us/blog/conversational-intelligence/201907/the-neuroscience-identity (archived at https://perma.cc/WQS2-4PDW)

# 03

# How to take control of reputation: strategy

*Here, we'll examine the steps to creating a powerful and sustainable reputation management strategy.*

Imagine you got into your car and headed for a destination you'd never been to before. You have an address and a time at which you need to arrive, but don't know the quickest way to get there. You want to avoid traffic and road construction and arrive on time, relaxed and ready. What would you do? Likely, you'd turn to your mobile phone or car's GPS system, enter the address where you're going and expect the GPS would offer you the fastest and shortest route there. A reputation management strategy is similar to a GPS system. When you're clear on where you're headed, which roadblocks you care about navigating and the state of mind in which to arrive, you can move forward in process, focused and intentional.

In this chapter, we'll look at how to build a reputation and personal brand strategy that empowers you to be clear on the destination you're pursuing, in charge of the opportunities you attract, confidently able to navigate roadblocks and obstacles, and ultimately able to build your desired reputation and legacy.

## Building a strategy is simple, but not easy

Building your strategy will likely be the hardest part of your personal branding journey. While personal brand is actually quite simple—there are no complicated formulas or intricate math equations—it's not easy. As we build your strategy, I will ask you questions that will likely make you uncomfortable and unsettled. They are simple questions that will require you to dig deep, to uncover your authentic assets, and to reflect on who you truly are and how you really want to live this gift you have called "life."

The hard work comes first because once you have a solid, sustainable and scalable personal branding strategy in place, you will see how manageable it is to direct your reputation to your advantage. Soon, you'll be making decisions using your strategy as a filter and finding that the choices you select are completely in alignment with where you *know* in your head, heart and gut you should be going. Your personal brand strategy becomes the organizing set of principles and the filtering process through which all decisions, relationships and communication must flow or get strained out. Just like an air filter prevents your furnace from blowing dirty, dusty and harmful air into your home, your personal brand strategy will ensure you live your life authentically, consistently and in the direction of your desired legacy.

## Reputation management gives you control

As with any strategy, first you'll examine where you are starting from, and then you'll decide where you want to go. When you decide what the beginning is, and what the end looks like, the strategy becomes the "how"—how will we get there? Your personal brand strategy will include several key factors, benchmarks and milestones, and goals designed to mature and evolve as you do. Unlike a formal business plan or product strategy, aspects of your personal brand strategy should be less fixed and more fluid, less linear and more circular. This often frustrates individuals trying to build a predictable and rigid plan for how their reputation can evolve and develop.

Most of us like control. I like control. Control over choices, decisions, relationships, behaviors, everything. If it can be controlled, I'd like to be the one controlling it. As humans, it's our nature to want to know what levers we have to work with, what the threats/options/choices are, and what we can control. When something is outside of our control, we might struggle, surrender or resist. Even the famous "Serenity Prayer" offers support to "accept the things I cannot change; the courage to change the things I can; and the wisdom to know the difference." It could be argued that we seek to understand what's in our power so that when something is outside our control, we have the peace of mind to let it go, release it, and stop trying to control it.

When you have an intentional personal brand strategy in place, you will feel in control. You'll see your path forward, believe you can navigate the risks and threats that might come, and feel empowered to live your life to the fullest. Personal branding gives you the "why" to filter decisions through, and that changes everything. You'll see that when you can't, in fact, control something, it's because it was either not meant for you or is not controllable.

Without control over your strategy and brand, here's what can happen:

- Your best clients forget to refer you.
- Employers look past your résumé and credentials.
- Your references ask what you'd like them to say about you in an endorsement.
- Your target audience can't articulate what makes you unique, or compelling, or relevant.

## Foundations of a strategy

Your personal brand strategy has several components which must integrate completely and work seamlessly together. You can't simply pick and choose the questions you want to answer and the areas you're willing to explore. It's all or nothing. Your personal brand strategy requires you to be consistent in the most authentic, intentional and constructive way possible. To promote your personal brand requires you to be an expert on you. No one will ever take as much time, effort or interest in figuring you out the way you need to. It's not because they don't care—they might care a lot! Your colleagues, staff, board might be passionately invested in your success, but they can't understand you at the deep and personal levels you can understand yourself. And this is the right way. When you're an expert on you, you are empowered to thoughtfully deliver your brand and value proposition to those target audiences who align with your values and vision. It's as simple as that. With the fundamentals of a brand strategy in place, the rest becomes manageable. To skip this step is costly, naïve and reckless. As with building a house, the framing, foundation, basic structure must be in place before you start picking out curtains and paint colors.

## Brand foundation: Values + action = credibility

### Credibility

Similar to a house construction, the foundation of a brand is credibility. To build a personal brand and grow reputation without credibility is futile, as audiences will perceive this as inauthentic and not trustworthy. Credibility means I trust you. It means I believe what you say, trust your vision, and will confidently put my own reputation (and credibility) on the line to refer and endorse you. Without credibility, I am reluctant, skeptical and hesitant. Always (even if feeling coerced by your status or position).

Consider the people in your life whom you trust and deem credible, such as your doctor, lawyer, financial advisor and babysitter. Are they credentialed? Likely. Do you know what they stand for, believe in and represent? Likely. Have you had experience interacting with them? Probably. Have they ever made a mistake or let you down? Maybe, but you still deem them credible because, overall, in the big picture of things, they act according to their values and you believe and trust in them. I have a financial advisor whom I trust implicitly. This person manages my investments, my business accounting, book-keeping—everything. And they've made mistakes which, fortunately, I caught before they were big. It happens. Human beings are capable of flaws and mistakes. But I trust this person with my money because they are credible and because, in the big picture of our relationship, they have shown themselves to be trustworthy.

## How to build credibility

If credibility is the foundation of your personal brand and anchors your reputation, how do you set out to become credible for specific traits, qualities or attributes? The answer is, again, simple, but not easy. The formula for credibility is: values + action = credibility. To be credible, your audience must know what you stand for and believe in (values) and see evidence (action) that you live accordingly. My financial advisor believes in taking care of their clients. When a mistake happens, they don't deny it, hide it, brush it off. They make sure my faith in them is intact, giving me plenty of time to explore the situation to ensure I'm comfortable before continuing.

### STEP 1: WHAT ARE YOUR VALUES?

When we talked about beliefs and judgments and perception in Chapter 1, we touched on values. Simply stated, your values are what you stand for, the criteria you use to make go/no-go, right/wrong, yes/no evaluations. When you feel that ache in your gut because you *know* you're about to make a mistake, that's typically when your values are being pushed against. Your values are often intertwined with the values you were taught by your parents, caregivers, teachers, friends, culture and community. Later, the values of your spouse, commanding officer, boss or industry leaders may blend into your value set, often making it hard to separate out your personal beliefs from those of the people you admire, respect and love, if needed. Most of us are so accustomed to incorporating the values of our community or loved ones that we adopt these values as our own until questioned.

Consider, for a moment, what you value. What do you hold dear as a value or principle? Really, really dig deep to think about a value you believe in so firmly that if that value were removed from you, you wouldn't be yourself. Did you come up with one, or two, or five?

An exercise I use in workshops to uncover values looks like this:

Take a stack of 10 index cards or scraps of paper and on each of them write one of your values. Just a word or two to describe the value you hold sacred. Lay the 10 cards or pieces of paper in front of you in no particular order.

Next, remove five. Take away five of the values you hold dear, leaving only the five most supremely valuable ones to you and your life. That was hard, wasn't it?

Now you're looking at your top five values—the beliefs and values you hold dear, that couldn't be separated from who you are, the values you use to determine what is right and what is wrong. The signposts of your morals and integrity.

Remove two more cards or pieces of paper, leaving only three values in front of you.

For most of us, this exercise causes us to question who we are, how we prioritize (what if I remove "family" from my values and leave "faith"? What kind of person will I be?) and what we hold sacred.

Looking at your top three values, what do you see? Is there anything consistent about the three you chose? Are they values that speak to your upbringing, education, training, cultural beliefs, faith? The beauty of values is that there is no right or wrong answer—the three values you see in front of you are the right ones for you. And that's what matters.

If you've previously not dug deep on your values, now would be the time. If you wrote words like "hard work" or "live with integrity," you'll need to unpack those. Oftentimes, I've found that it takes several iterations of this exercise to reduce and refine one's values to the most foundational level. If you're struggling with this, that's normal.

I recall a workshop where a participant shared his value as "integrity." The definition of "integrity" seemed obvious to him, so he declared it to the group with confidence. I inquired, "What does integrity mean to you?" He looked at me dumbfounded as if I should know. "Integrity," he continued, "means always doing the right thing." Fair enough, I thought. But I pushed, "Please continue. Explain more." Frustrated, he then declared, "Ma'am, integrity is always doing the right thing when you're told." And there it was—his definition of integrity was not the same as mine—or maybe yours—but to him it was crystal clear. When he was told to do something, he'd always do it. And furthermore, he inferred it would always be the right thing to do.

Again, the goal is not that I tell you which values to live by or that you focus on ones that are trendy or on point. Your values are the ones so deep inside yourself that they are blatantly obvious to you and you can confidently live your life through and with them at all times. I found it funny when an audience member once asked if I could just "list the values that are best to promote ourselves with," but it's not that simple. Your values are yours and yours alone, and they must be clear.

When I did this exercise for myself, in 2008, I knew I'd need to be clear on my values to be able to build and promote a business that could sustain and scale. I knew that I had to find a narrative that would allow me to expand and shrink my offering as needed, would give my colleagues, staff, clients and stakeholders confidence in me, and one which would empower me to clearly navigate the turbulence of growing a new business. I also recognized that my values, if publicly promoted as part of my visible brand, would be scrutinized and I'd have to be accountable to them.

After introspection similar to the exercise above, and after considering all the values I hold dear and live by, I landed on two specific values through which every decision, hire, client engagement and promotion would need to fit for me: gratitude and generosity. When I considered my values and what I simply could not work without, those two words stood out as clear. Saying "yes" to volunteer or pro bono engagements filters through my generosity value. Finding ways to share or donate (time, expertise, money) is easy when I can express my gratitude for all I've been given and the freedoms I enjoy as a woman, entrepreneur and American. Those two values are what all the decisions in my life pivot around, not just in business.

Whether you land on two, or three, or five values through which your personal brand will live, know them well. Be specific, even granular, about what the values represent to you, how they impact you, how they make you feel, and then build confidence as you begin to share those values with others. In just a moment, you'll be asked to apply action to them to be perceived as credible.

### STEP 2: ACTIONS

Your values are the first part of the formula, but then come the actions. It might seem like actions would be the easier step, since you just have to act according to what you believe. But it's not that simple. Your actions are proof and evidence of your values; they show how you walk the talk on what you claim to believe in, fight for and support. Values without proof are not meaningful. When values are demonstrated, shown, proven and seen in action, they are assigned credibility.

Imagine the politician who promises their support of an underserved population. They stand in front of their constituents and declare they will do everything in their power to help these people, because it's what the politician believes in, will fight for: values. But, if there's no evidence of this kind of advocacy in the politician's past, if their constituents haven't seen them previously try to help or endorse programs that will help, their vows are met with hesitancy and cynicism.

The twist to the formula is that simply acting according to your values is often not enough to earn credibility and trust. As we all know, everyone is busy, and people aren't paying close attention to everything you do. If you act according to your values, but you don't promote why you're doing so, others might miss the attachment of actions to values. Yes, I'm saying you need to let people know *why* you're doing what you're doing when you're acting in alignment with your values. As uncomfortable as that sounds, here's how this works.

When I was clear on my two primary values—gratitude and generosity—I sought to express those values wherever I could find the chance. I helped, mentored, donated and volunteered to show my gratefulness for all I had in life. In 2009, I was made aware of the challenge military veterans experience as they transition from a military to a civilian career and realized I could help. Gratitude (for their service) and generosity (I have valuable skills and information that can help) led me to reach out to military organizations, non-profits and private transition groups where I offered to donate my expertise in personal branding and reputation management to give transitioning service members valuable skills they needed to successfully reintegrate into the civilian sector.

The problem was that I had zero credibility. I was an unknown in a very insulated, self-protecting and skeptical community (there are civilians who tried to capitalize on helping veterans). Without credibility, most doors closed in my face. After months of trying, a door opened. A group in Philadelphia allowed me to come and teach transitioning service members (mostly Special Forces) about personal branding. The program was a hit! After a few training sessions, I began traveling to Philadelphia a few times a year, closing my business during that time so I could teach uninterrupted. As a new company, I'm not sure about the soundness of the business decision, but my credibility within the military community, as someone who was passionate about gratitude and generosity, grew.

I began writing articles for leading military and business publications about transition, the business case for hiring veterans, and pushing for support of those in the transition process. Many times, I self-funded my books, coaching services and travel costs to participate in events where I could teach the personal branding process to active duty service members, veterans and military spouses. It was my way of saying, "thank you for your service." Each time I stood in front of a group of service members, or spoke to hiring managers about the veteran employee, or even when I stood on the famous red "dot" in my 2016 TEDx Talk, I needed to explicitly connect my value to my action and state that I was there because of my values—gratitude and generosity (also happens to be the name of my TEDx Talk). Quickly, my credibility grew exponentially, and I was invited to speak at large conventions and events, I authored three books on military transition, and began speaking in international media, advocating for veterans in transition. I knew that in order to have the kind of reach and visibility I needed to create the broad and deep impact I wanted to make in the military community, I'd need to lead with my values. But I didn't take the steps in order to get credit, accolades or praise. Those come with credibility. Credibility doesn't show up because you want it or believe you deserve it. It's a result of living in your values. Tie your action to your values at every opportunity.

At this point, you may be thinking, "but that sounds like arrogance… or bragging. If you do good things, that you're led to do because of your values, others should just know it." Unfortunately, that's not how it works. Here's an example of what could happen: Bruce runs a large, global company. He arrives at the office early in the morning and typically works well past dinner. Bruce loves his job, but even more than that, he loves helping people. His value set pivots around a passion for *helping people reach their potential, even when they don't believe in themselves*. Bruce mentors several emerging leaders in his company, volunteers with The Boys and Girls Club in his community, and coaches graduating college students through a youth-to-hire program at a local non-profit. He even works as a volunteer umpire for a high school youth program in his area. Bruce lights up when he's serving and helping people grow their skills, confidence and competence.

You might think that anyone who sees how hard Bruce works, observes him mentoring employees at the office and sees him coaching youth in his community would recognize how much he loves to help. But, is there another possible narrative? Could an observer conclude that maybe Bruce spends so much time helping youth in his community because he has a bad home life and looks for reasons to avoid going home to his family? Could they deduce that mentoring staff at the office is part of his work responsibilities or that he doesn't hire people with adequate training? If Bruce fails to tell us why he does these things, it's possible to perceive his action differently.

Instead, as Bruce begins to introduce subtle and consistent messaging into his actions, he drives credibility. When a mentee thanks him for his time reviewing their career goals, he replies, "My pleasure. I'm passionate about helping professionals reach their goals and really enjoy our work together!" As he continues to serve with youth in his community, Bruce weaves through a narrative of, "I'm honored to have spent the day with you all today. It's important to me to help you reach your goals and dreams. That motivates me!" Slowly, but clearly, Bruce begins to be recognized and referred to as the important business leader who is *passionate about helping people reach their potential.*

## Assessment phase

### *Step 1: Benchmarking your current brand*

As mentioned before, building a personal brand requires deep self-assessment and introspection. The first step after clarifying your values is to understand where your brand is today. We call this your current brand. The tricky part of assessing current brand is that our judgment and beliefs about how it should be, or how we wish it to be, flood in. We want to be seen as warm, thoughtful, collaborative, but sometimes that's not the case. Or, at least, those aren't the exact words others might use to describe you, today.

Begin by thinking about feedback or comments you've received about how you're currently perceived:

- How have people described you when presenting you? For example, if someone introduces you as, "This is Mary—she's a riot when you get a few drinks in her!" that's good insight into how that person perceives you. Similarly, if you've been introduced only by your title, "This is Scott, he runs the place…" or by your credentials, "I'd like to introduce you to Marvin, he's got two master's degrees and a PhD in biochemistry, so he's smart," it's worth noting.

- Consider formal feedback assessments, such as 360 evaluations or board reviews. Were there themes around how you're perceived revealed in the feedback? If you're commonly referred to in a certain way, can you identify a pattern of impressions you're making? For instance, my client Patricia routinely received evaluations and feedback from her staff and board of directors. Consistently, those offering input noted her decisiveness, consideration and ability to take calculated risks. They called these "her strengths." They also shared that she limited the input she received from her peers and employees prior to making a decision, causing them to wonder if her scope was limited. While she was decisive in her actions, her staff and board were concerned that she received enough varied input to make an informed decision. No one said this directly, but enough of the feedback hinted and implied as such, giving Patricia and I the insight we needed to make this assessment and conclude how she was currently perceived.

- This last one might surprise you, but have you heard any gossip about how you come across? Even water-cooler banter can hint at how you are perceived. Imagine you hear that your colleagues don't include you in group social outings and events because they don't think you'd enjoy them, that you "lack a fun gene" and could bring the group down emotionally. While hurtful to hear, this kind of insight can tell you that you're coming across as standoffish and unapproachable.

Take the input you've received to date—through formal or informal measures—and categorize the findings into several areas:

- opportunities to grow and improve;
- weaknesses and risks;
- threats to your brand;
- areas to exploit.

This becomes a baseline for your personal brand strategy.

Try to resist the temptation to judge how your brand looks today. You might assess that your current reputation is short of ideal, that you're not seen favorably or that you really aren't regarded for the values you want to be credible for. That's okay. Your work has just begun, and we need to know where we're starting from. That's all this exercise is: establishing baseline.

## Step 2: The importance of feedback and input

Perhaps you don't have a sense of how you're perceived by others, or you want to test your perception against what their actual feelings might be about who you are, what you care about and the value you add. Maybe you don't receive formal assessments as part of your job. Feedback is a great way to do this.

The process I use at LIDA360 runs the gamut of light feedback surveying to deep perception mapping studies on clients. I created the methodology to ensure my clients' self-evaluation is accurate and goals are realistic, given various parameters and timeframes. The feedback surveys we deploy for clients are designed to help us determine how close, or far, the client is from where they are today and where they want to get.

To do a survey yourself and assess your current personal brand, consider using an email form to ask trusted advisors, influencers and stakeholders several open-ended questions about you. Brand survey questions could include:

- What are five words that come to mind when you think of me and my reputation?
- If you were to refer me to an opportunity, what kind of opportunity would it be and why would you refer me?
- What do you believe I'm passionate about?
- What makes me unique and memorable?
- For what would you consult with me or seek my advice on?

These questions give clues beyond just a yes/no response. They're also designed not to entice a flood of negative feedback (in my experience, it rarely happens that someone views your request for feedback as an opportunity to open the floodgates of hatred towards you). You'll be looking for patterns around how you add value, where you've built deep relationships (and where the relationship might be more superficial?), whether someone is comfortable transferring credibility to you in the form of an endorsement or referral, and more. When I interpret feedback for my clients, I leverage years of understanding responses from many decades of asking and assessing quality and quantity of perception input to identify the patterns of opportunity. For yourself, simply look at the answers offered and read into them the opportunities you can pursue.

Asking for feedback requires finesse. Resist blasting your LinkedIn connections with the request for personal feedback. Instead, choose recipients whom you believe will trust you enough with the information, and whom you trust will be honest and forthcoming. Be sure to frame up the request by acknowledging that this feedback is meaningful to you and how you'll be able to grow value in your community. Acknowledge that you trust them, and their insight, and value their insights. When responses come to you, and assuming you deployed the survey yourself (and didn't hire a third person), say "thank you." Do not retort, argue, make excuses for or correct their feedback. They have shown vulnerability in sharing their views, and if you respond with defensive posture, you may damage the relationship permanently. Instead, when you ask for feedback and receive it, respond with gratitude. Later, as you build out your brand and put the feedback into action, it's acceptable (and sometimes encouraged) to return to the respondents with an update. Let them know you've been working on the changes they suggested and would value their opinion on your progress. Now you've started a healthy and ongoing personal development dialogue.

Enlisting others to give you feedback on your reputation and brand is terrifying for most professionals. We aren't asking them to assess competency or skills, but rather to evaluate you based on their perception of your behavior, their judgment about you as a person, and their beliefs about your life and contribution. How scary! Actually, soliciting feedback on your personal brand is truly one of the most remarkable and insightful steps in the process. Most of my clients scoff at the idea initially, then revel and delight in the discoveries and insights they receive. Sometimes, the feedback points out blind spots and weaknesses ("I didn't realize I avoided eye contact when I spoke to people," or, "No one noted that I'm passionate about advancing social justice. How could they not know that about me?") which may need to be mitigated and overcome to build a solid and scalable brand.

In other cases, the feedback reveals opportunity. I remember working with a talented and knowledgeable woman who led a large non-profit in Europe. Her group's mission served disenfranchised children with innovative tools and learning to help them out of the cycle of poverty. My client, Clarise, was extraordinarily passionate about her work and was considered an expert in the fields of social change, childhood development and community activism. Clarise was also very tall and striking in her appearance (her long, flowing red hair almost screamed to be let out of the tight bun she kept it in at all times). She refused to call attention to herself and downplayed her appearance to focus all attention on the message: serving the children.

After her initial intake session, we deployed her feedback surveys and the results were mostly consistent with what we expected: She was well regarded for her leadership of the cause, her knowledge and advocacy, and her scholarly speeches inspired others to want to help alongside her. What surprised Clarise, however, was the feedback that came in about her appearance. Several surveys pointed to the notion that she depreciated the value of her looks to draw attention towards her (and therefore the cause). The surveys noted how she should use her height and striking presence to show empowerment of the message, to confidently own her voice and to make herself more memorable. She could be a role model to the children, as well, if she proudly and confidently leveraged her appearance along with her message. These respondents weren't trivializing her looks or encouraging her to "play up" her appearance and sexualize the message, but rather they felt that downplaying her physical assets could actually be hurting her credibility and power.

This surprised Clarise, but she was willing to consider the input and we crafted a plan to move her towards a more confident and visible presence. Slowly, she experimented with a little makeup, she let her hair down, pinning up just the sides to be most comfortable on stage. She began pushing her shoulders back and filling up her entire six-foot frame. There were even occasions where I saw her wear high heels. Clarise used the feedback to empower her sense of self, to grow into the woman she needed to be, to serve her cause and mission not only professionally but also personally. She began to like who she saw in the mirror and not to fear it would detract from her intelligence or her important message. She realized she could be powerful (intelligent, thoughtful, innovative), confident and attractive in building her credibility. Her organization grew, her confidence grew, and her impact on her community grew exponentially.

*Step 3: Visualizing the ideal brand state: Creating a desired brand*

Remember when I said having a personal brand strategy and game plan gives you more control than you could ever imagine? Here's where that happens: How do you want to be remembered? What legacy do you desire to leave behind? How do you want people to perceive you? Imagine the end of your life and the people you worked with, served, mentored, hired/fired and grew with are all reflecting on your life and work. In an ideal situation, what should they feel? What sentiments flood their emotions? Resist focusing on what you did— such as "grew the company from an idea to viability"—and instead focus on how you made them all feel. Brands are feelings, remember?

When you imagine the ideal end state, what feelings are these people experiencing as they remember you? Are they happy, remembering that you always took time to help them when they were struggling? Are they inspired, reflecting on how you, a thoughtful innovator, took the time to share your ideas and collaborate with others? Will they feel proud to have known you, reflecting on your generosity towards others, and the gratitude you filled your heart, work and contributions with?

Your desired brand is where you get control. This is where you take ownership of how you want to be perceived and how you'll ultimately be remembered. Taking inventory of your life and relationships, your desired brand is the embodiment of your legacy, and how you will have lived a life with purpose, intention and impact.

When we talk about legacy, it's helpful to remember the story[1] of Alfred Nobel. As the inventor of dynamite, and with a father who was an engineer in the Crimean War, Nobel's work in explosives made him the very wealthy owner of nearly 100 factories that made explosives and munitions, and his name was typically associated with war and not peace. When his brother, Ludvig, died, a French newspaper mistakenly reported Albert passed. The erroneous obituary "branded him a 'merchant of death' who had grown rich by developing new ways to 'mutilate and kill.'" Albert, it is believed, became obsessed with the way he would be remembered posthumously and set out to change his legacy. He launched the Nobel Prize, and left most of his fortune to supporting those who changed the world for the better.

Most likely you won't have an opportunity to see how your obituary will read. If, in some way, you could read it, would you be proud of how your life was summed up? Right now, right here, you have an opportunity to change the trajectory of your life and to positively influence and design the legacy you will leave behind when you are gone. Legacy might feel like a weighty topic at this point in your life and career. You might be reading this while in your 20s or 40s or even 60s and consider your legacy a far-off, distant ideal. You might be reading this as a senior, concerned you won't have enough time left to positively effect change. "Start from where you are" were words spoken to me as I started out on my journey of personal branding. These words tell us that whatever has come before, whatever mistakes or missteps we've made, we can go forward. Forgiving ourselves is key, but so is having a plan to move into the future. With a clear and concise vision of how we want to be remembered, we can craft a personal brand that is authentic, tangible and memorable, offering us great rewards and opportunities along the way.

The other important note about ideal or desired brand is that it doesn't enable you to create a reputation you're not capable of or qualified for. I see this struggle every day. Years ago, a successful sales trainer was referred to me by a colleague I truly respect. The referring friend told me this client would be a challenge. "Their view of what's possible is a bit skewed," she said. Still, I felt I could help this person see what's possible and what isn't and make them into another success story. Unfortunately, this was my first client relationship that went sideways: He truly wanted to build a personal brand and reputation for himself as a charismatic, engaging and lively sales trainer. His role model was Tony Robbins. "That's who I know I'm meant to be exactly like!" he professed. After our first meeting I realized he was far from the personality or charisma of Tony Robbins.

This man's style, delivery and personality were calculated, somber, systematic and effective. He taught complex sales methodology and empowered his audiences to follow structured systems which delivered calculated and measurable results. In terms of personality, he reminded me of Ben Stein's character, the professor, in *Ferris Bueller's Day Off* asking, "Anyone? Anyone?" You get the picture. The perception mapping feedback we received confirmed where his value laid—his clients loved him and hired and referred him often. They appreciated his direct, straightforward style of delivery, which yielded results within their sales teams. What this man had was working—he was constantly booked and praised. Yet he wanted a style he admired, which was not genuine to himself. After using every tool and resource I knew of to convince him that my branding techniques could not turn him into Tony Robbins, we parted ways and I learned a valuable lesson about expectation-setting.

## Step 4: Strategically evaluating and using the feedback

When you evaluated your personal brand feedback, or perhaps you deployed a personal brand survey yourself, you looked for patterns: What is currently working/not working? Does the feedback indicate I'm on track for my desired reputation? Where do I have to do work to ensure my legacy is intact? The feedback identifies if there is a gap between how you're perceived today and how you want to be perceived (legacy), or not. In some cases, the gap is large, and your personal brand strategy will include robust strategic ways to close that gap and align who you are with who you want to be seen as. In other cases, your feedback may reveal that you're actually a lot closer to your desired brand than previously believed. In that instance, you'll want a personal brand strategy that amplifies and supports the brand assets that make you valued.

Given that the feedback is to guide your strategy, not all feedback needs to be acted on. The goal is to get to your ideal, desired reputation. If your feedback offers input and suggestions that could pull you off that track or don't support your desired brand, they don't have to be acted upon. For example, if my desired brand is to be remembered for my two primary values, gratitude and generosity, and my legacy goal is to be known as *someone who gave back much more than she took*, then feedback that mentions my large personality (implied as a negative) is not necessarily worthy of fixing. Maybe I leverage my boldness to make it known that people need helping? Perhaps my over-the-top style is what garners attention so I can make a greater impact in the lives of those I serve? "Large personality" is not necessarily a weakness.

But, if I received feedback that I was standoffish and withheld helping others with my knowledge or talents, that would be feedback directly inconsistent with my desired brand goals. That feedback would definitely need to be corrected, because someone who is perceived as unwilling to help others, who won't share their gifts and talents and who is unapproachable, is not someone who *gives back much more than she takes.*

## Identifying your target audience

Until now we've been talking about you; after all, it is your personal brand. But there is another half of the strategy we must consider: your target audience. Think of the target audience as the people who must care. Your target audience are the people who must find you relevant, interesting and compelling because they have the opportunities you seek.

If you were marketing a luxury sports car, you'd have to be very clear on who your target audience was. You'd invest money and time and effort marketing your product to them, encouraging them to test drive, creating an experience of car ownership, pointing out relevant features and assets, and so on. You would not spend resources marketing your automobile to teenagers who can't afford your car, or people in areas where they don't drive, or to individuals who turn their noses up at luxury items. You'd find your audience and promote to them, in their language, in the way they get excited. Your target audience, in this case, has the means and desire to spend the kind of money necessary to buy your luxury car.

Similarly, as individuals, we must be clear on who we're targeting. This part feels risky: By eliminating some people from our target set, are we limiting our options? What if someone who isn't our target audience still wants to hire us, buy from us, invest with us? That certainly can, and does, happen. But we aren't spending our resources and effort marketing to them. We market to the ones who are looking for someone exactly like us!

Here are some examples of target audiences:

- If you're looking for a new job, your target audience might include executive recruiters, influential networking relations, contacts who currently work in your desired industry or company, references who can speak to your track record and career, and so on.

- If you're seeking investment for your venture or company, your target audience could include key financial prospects, members of your executive team who will endorse and refer you, strategic media who blog or cover your industry or sector, current and previous employees who can say nice things about you and your leadership in high-visibility online forums, etc.

- If you're embarking on a career as a solopreneur or consultant, your target audience might include strategic business allies and partners who can refer clients and resources to you, staff you might hire or contract with, who will elevate your marketing and positioning, potential clients who will want to hire you, past clients who've worked favorably with you, and more.

Your target audience can change based on your situation—as in, moving from jobseeker to employed professional yields a different focus—but they won't change dramatically. The people you get along best with, who understand and value your opinions and perspectives, who are looking to engage with, refer and endorse you, typically don't change in type of person; they may just change in terms of the role they fulfill in your strategy.

### Your target audience persona

Your target audience is the individual or group of individuals to whom your brand needs to be relevant and compelling. As such, you need to be clear on what this audience needs and wants. You should know who your target audience is, what they do, where they are located and what they care about. Start by listing their titles, names, identifications or job descriptions. In the example above, if you're in a job search, you might list hiring managers or executive recruiters. Consider geography—are you looking to relocate, build your brand globally or pivot your reputation within the company? Knowing where your target audience is located is vital.

Finally, you should focus most of your attention on what they need to know and what they want to feel to see you as relevant and compelling. We call these needs their functional needs and emotional needs. As human beings, we need to know certain things about you in order to have the conversation (functional needs). If I'm hiring an executive coach, I need to know they have training, credentials, track record and maybe some clients I can speak to about their work. But human beings are also feelings-driven (emotional needs). Previously, we talked about how important emotions are to the branding process, and here's why: Your target audience needs to feel certain things towards you. Perhaps they need to feel safe, valued, validated or supported. These feelings, if not present, will make it almost impossible to build a relationship with your audience. Unless you are the absolute only solution in the world, and they have no other choice but to engage with you, feelings matter. While I might be impressed by an executive coach's pedigree, training and client list, if they creep me out or I don't feel they'll understand or relate to me, I'll keep looking. We make decisions when both our functional and emotional needs are met.

Start by making two lists. On the top of one write "Functional" and on the other write "Emotional." Then, list the needs, as you believe them to be, of your target audience. What do they need to know about you to engage with you? Which credentials, services, deliverables and past experiences do they need to be confident you possess before they'll entertain feeling something for you?

Next, under the heading of "Emotional," list what you believe this audience needs to feel from you. What do they care about? What's important to them? Get as specific on both sets of lists as you can.

Often, the first list is easiest. When I train on this with sales teams, they list functional needs of potential clients quickly and swiftly: "They need to know we offer competitive pricing, that our clients have been with us a long time, that our sales staff is constantly trained on new technology, and that our leadership has a transparent view into each salesperson's work…" But then, I ask, what do your clients need to feel? (This is typically where we spend much more of our time because the answers aren't as easy or forthcoming!) Eventually, we might uncover that their potential and current clients need to feel, "I won't leave them hanging, no matter what problem arises. I won't make them feel stupid if they ask a basic question. I really care about their business, and will help them think through buying decisions, even if that means they buy from a competitor."

You've likely guessed where this exercise is heading: If you give your clients what they need functionally and emotionally, they will buy from you and stay loyal. In personal branding, which is emotion-driven, we cannot just position ourselves as satisfying half the needs of our audience. We must deliver what they need to know, and what they need to feel, in order to be relevant and compelling to them.

## Action phase

With an assessment of where your reputation and brand are currently, the vision for the desired reputation you'll work towards, feedback on how close or far apart you are today from where you want to be, and a clear picture of who you're targeting to influence, inspire and impact, you're ready to assemble a game plan, a strategy, to bring your personal brand to life. You've actually just done the hardest part. Looking inward is not easy. Getting clear on who you are as a person, the legacy you want to leave, and the people you'll seek to build relationship with takes great effort.

Now, let's set a strategy for how the various assets available to you will work in concert to return the results you're after. If your goal is to become more visible and known, there's a strategy for that. If you'll be pivoting your career and want to retain the brand assets that served you before in your new focus, there's a strategy for that. And there's a strategy when things go wrong and you need to get your name back and repair and rebuild your reputation.

### Step 1

First, assemble the pieces you've identified. Clearly and simply list responses this way:

MY CURRENT BRAND

I'm known for:

What makes me unique and memorable today is:

People come to me for advice about:

What makes me stand apart from my competitors is:

I'm introduced as:

MY DESIRED BRAND

I want to be remembered for:

I will leave a legacy of:

I want people to remember me for:

I will have made the people I serve feel:

### MY FEEDBACK REFLECTED THESE PATTERNS, TRENDS AND TRAITS

Positive feedback:

Negative feedback:

Areas to focus on to get to desired brand:

Feedback that surprised me:

Feedback that delighted me:

### MY TARGET AUDIENCE

Whom do I seek to influence, inspire and impact?

How will my target audience serve me (what opportunities can they afford me)?

Where is my target audience located?

What do they need functionally?

What do they need emotionally?

### Step 2

Now, look at those lists. What strikes you? Is the gap between where you are and where you want to be wide or narrow? What key words or key phrases pop out at you? Are they the same words or phrases your target audience uses to seek you out?

### Step 3

With the information you've gathered, and a vision for where you're headed, inventory your current promotion tactics:

- **How are you showing up on social media?** Is your digital reputation in alignment with your desired reputation? We'll unpack this more when we evaluate how to use each tactic, but for now, evaluate where you are today. Take into consideration the number of active followers you have, how much engagement you get when you post or comment, which platforms you're most active on and any feedback you've received on how you present yourself online.

- **How do you speak about yourself?** Are you strategic and clear in how you express your value when you meet someone new? Are you reinforcing positive self-talk when you're alone? What narrative are others sharing about who you are, what you care about and where you add value? Take note of any patterns or habits you've fallen into when speaking about yourself to others.

- **Are you projecting a confident and consistent image in how you dress and how you enter a room?** Is your wardrobe a reflection of your stature and influence? Do you carry yourself with confidence and self-appreciation? Have you taken a look at your wardrobe, hairstyle, glasses and other image pieces you use to create an impression of yourself? Have you worked with a stylist?

- **Are the people you surround yourself with—your network online and in person—supporting and enhancing your reputation, or detracting?** Are they in positions to help you, and where you can return the favor? How do you maintain your contact lists (online, on the computer, on your mobile phone, on paper)? How often do you assess and purge your networking contacts and strategically add new ones?

The goal is to build a strategy that leverages what's working and corrects what isn't. If your desired reputation requires endorsement, testimony and referrals, relationship-building may be your focus. If repairing your personal brand will mean altering and affecting the first three pages of a Google search on you, then digital capital may take precedence.

## Step 4

Clarify your goals. Your desired brand is the ultimate goal, but what goals and milestones will you need to achieve to build this legacy? Break down your desired brand goal into smaller steps. It might look like this (the text in brackets represents how someone might personalize the template):

> To be known as (a passionate and committed thought leader) in (my firm/industry/community) I will first establish credibility for these values (integrity, my faith in God, and lifting up other people). I will contribute to my industry by (volunteering to mentor young professionals, speaking at industry conferences, writing a book about my upbringing and overcoming challenges), sharing my voice, knowledge and expertise.
>
> Next, I will focus on relationships with (my colleagues at work) to enhance my own credibility and to contribute to their effort (which supports my own). We will collaborate on stage, in publications, in person and online.
>
> I will carry myself this way (with confidence, presence and openness), presenting an image of someone who is committed to (being approachable, thoughtful and compassionate).
>
> Ultimately, the target audience I seek to influence, inspire and impact (my co-workers, industry partners and community leaders) will see me as (someone who leads by example, lives through integrity, and is faithful to God and family).

## In closing

One of the most remarkable and common responses I receive when teaching personal branding is that it is hard and intense at the outset, but then self-marketing and self-promotion feel absurdly simple afterwards. That's exactly the point! When someone attempts to build a solid and referable reputation without a strategy, everything feels random and abstract: Should I write a recommendation for that person on LinkedIn? How should I be introduced to the audience before I take the stage? Should I wear a suit and tie or jeans and a blazer? What do I do with my hands? All decisions about how to present oneself feel like they're made in a vacuum of context.

Instead, when a personal branding strategy is in place, decisions become easier. You know how to show up, what to say (and not say) and who to pursue for a professional, mutually beneficial relationship. The answers lie in your strategy.

Your strategy is a finely tuned symphony of what you believe in and stand for (values) layered nicely with how you want to be remembered (ideal brand state). The starting point is here, now, and the end point is legacy. In between are the steps, actions, relationships and judgments that form perception and afford you the opportunities you desire.

## Endnote

1  Andrews, E (2016) Did a premature obituary inspire the Nobel Prize?, *History*, https://www.history.com/news/did-a-premature-obituary-inspire-the-nobel-prize (archived at https://perma.cc/5TEV-8D8Q)

# 04

# How to take control of reputation: tactics

*With a strategy in hand, it's time to build out the tactics, steps and cadence of implementing a personal brand program to enhance reputation and gain visibility.*

In the last chapter, we discussed the importance of having a game plan and a strategy for building and living your personal brand. Now, let's discuss the tactical assets you'll need to consistently and confidently deploy to drive a positive reputation with your target audiences. I'll share the four key areas of tactical expression of personal branding that ensure your reputation allows you to influence, inspire and impact others in the ways you seek. While we might regret and hold blame for things we've done, or failed to do, in our past, what's happened is history. What's yet to come is our potential. Building a personal brand strategy, with thoughtful and integrated tactics, gives you control over the future. Whether you are returning to work after raising children, retiring after a long career in business, or trying to recover from a mistake which threatens your future career and ability to provide for your family, it's critical to remember that you will now be driving the outcome of your career by intentionally and thoughtfully managing your strategy and tactics.

## Operating from a fixed versus a growth mindset

In personal branding, someone operating with a fixed mindset might believe, "I'm an analytical person. I'll never be seen as creative." Or, "My experiences show me to be an introvert. I'm not good at meeting new people." They believe their traits are set and therefore new ideas are thwarted, growth is "managed," and innovation is often perceived as a risk. Someone coming from a growth mindset, on the other hand, perceives new ideas and innovation as exciting and worth pursuing because they see potential in new opportunities. A fixed mindset leads you to believe things are set and must be worked with as is. A growth mindset sees the possibility and prospects! To fully embrace and deploy the following tactics, it will be vital that you explore growth mindset thinking. If you believe you operate from a fixed mindset, try to open up your thinking. Envision possibilities where roadblocks may be present, open yourself to new ideas and ways of thinking, and be willing to promote yourself and your value in creative and innovative ways to get the attention of the audiences you seek to influence, inspire and impact.

## Setting goals and clarifying your vision

Before we dive into the tactics you'll use to build and scale your reputation and personal brand, it's important to note that these aren't menu options: You can't simply pick the one or two tactics that feel easiest or most comfortable to you and ignore the rest. Each of these tactics must integrate with the rest of your narrative to provide a complete picture of who you are, what you value and what you can offer. For example, let's say you focus only on building your digital reputation. What happens when someone meets you and who you are in person falls short of what they believed true about you online? Your brand will suffer.

Admittedly, some tactics will be more immediately relevant for you than others, depending on where you are in your career and reputation management strategy. For example, if you are working to repair a negative reputation or build your voice in a new market, you might need to focus more on generating content and distributing that content online and in respected publications. That doesn't mean you should avoid meeting new people or stop working on your value proposition or discontinue paying attention to your image and body language. When practiced together, the tactics described below form a synchronized system that also allows for the practice of individual tactics as needed. This makes building your personal brand manageable. If I were to suggest you focus all of your time and effort on building out each of these tactics with equal force, you might give up from exhaustion, or worry that you'd have to employ a team of professionals to help you.

Here's an example of how this works: John is an aerospace executive I coached. When I first met him, he expressed this goal: "I'm good at what I do, have an impressive résumé and set of credentials, but I keep being passed over for a leadership position. I want to be working in a senior executive role by the time I'm 45 years old." John knew his skills were sharp, he'd received awards and certifications to verify his tactical knowledge of the programs he led, but he lacked what was needed for company leadership to see him as a leader. To build his personal brand strategy, John needed to first focus on his relationships inside the company and build credibility with his sponsors and internal advocates to elevate his reputation. With a firm understanding of what his company leaders considered "leadership material," John also needed to be seen as respected in the industry. He focused on publishing papers in leading industry journals and spoke at industry conferences. We worked on his executive presence and body language, as his posture and wardrobe hadn't evolved much since he left graduate school.

John had a long list of tactics towards his ambitious goal. However, they were manageable and strategic when stacked in an order that made his plan workable given his busy schedule. One by one, as John gained traction in an area, and was becoming noticed, he shifted focus to another area. Soon, all the areas he needed bench strength in were operating at high volume, and John was put on track for senior leadership at his company. Had I tried to bury him with "to do" lists and overwhelmed him with ideas, he would have flamed out and become discouraged. John knew he needed to improve many aspects of his brand and positioning, and we focused on what got the most attention and recognition—building on his values to earn him credibility—before adding more emphasis to the next area. John viewed his effort as a concert, where he needed all instruments playing in harmony, but sometimes one performer got a solo or two to grow stronger.

## Application phase

In Figure 4.1, you can see each of the tactics we'll be reviewing as part of the implementation and action of your personal brand to build your desired reputation. When your target audience sees you showing up consistently through the practice of these tactics, they will perceive you as someone who lives in alignment with their values and be reassured that you are to be trusted. Then, they can confidently and enthusiastically refer and endorse you. When these actions

FIGURE 4.1    Personal branding tactics

are in conflict with what you say you believe in, support and advocate for, your target audience grows suspicious and over time will believe you can't be trusted.

As you read through the list of tactics, consider what you're doing today that supports or detracts from the desired personal brand you're building towards. Examine how consistent or inconsistent you're being, whether you've paid attention to your behavior and if there's room for growth (likely there will be). Resist being too hard on yourself. Many very successful individuals aren't clear on the recipe for success they deployed, only that they want to ensure it is replicable.

## Narrative and communication: Driving influence through language

As someone who loves to write, it's natural I'd love language. But I love narrative even more than language, because narrative is storytelling. When we shape, develop and share narrative, we can use language to meet our own goals as well as the needs of the specific audience we wish to attract. From early childhood we're taught through stories, which teach us about right and wrong, good and evil, dreams and misfortune. We frame our experiences and share them with others by telling stories. "Let me tell you what happened to me!" begins many of the stories we tell about our lives. These stories let people glimpse who we are, what's happened to us, and why we deem it all meaningful.

Stories are also at the heart of personal brands. Your brand should tell the story of why you are here, why you matter and why you care (and, why you want us to care, too). If you aren't controlling your narrative, you leave too much to chance and speculation. When you control the narrative, you drive the audience to the conclusion you desire them to reach.

*Narrative starts with self-talk*

To effectively build, pivot or repair your reputation, you need to focus on three distinct aspects of your narrative: what you tell yourself, what you tell other people, and what other people share about you. The story you tell yourself is self-talk. Self-talk impacts how you come across to others, and then, ultimately, how others speak of you when you're not in the room. More and more, the coaching work I'm doing with personal branding clients emphasizes self-talk—the powerful messages we tell ourselves that either build us up and give us confidence or tear us down and fill our psyche with shame, guilt and a sense of inadequacy. Across all levels of business, entrepreneurship, global industry, professionals of all ranks and status are telling themselves messages like:

· I don't deserve to be happy.
· They'll never pick me.
· Who do I think I am to compete for that opportunity?
· I'm not worthy.
· I should just quit now. I'll look foolish if I continue.

As well as:

· I've got this!
· I'm ready!
· This is what I've worked so hard for!
· I believe in me, and they'll believe in me, too!
· This is my purpose for being here!

Perhaps one reason self-talk is so critical is because we hear these words in our own voice, in our own dialect and language. There is no filtering through misinterpretation—our internal vocal system is saying this, so it must be true, we believe. There are numerous courses, seminars and books written on the power of positive self-talk which advocate for mantras designed to reconfigure our outlook on life by repeating words in a cadence and order that build up positive feelings and squash the negative. There is no shortage of information available online about the power of self-talk and why it's so important to focus on reminding yourself of what you're grateful for, what's good and worthy about you, and why your personal mission is unique and valuable.

For personal branding purposes, self-talk is critical for another reason: Self-talk frames the narrative you'll build a reputation around. You must believe what will be written about you on the company's website, in your own books, and in your own mission statement. You must be confident in the qualities you'll be known for and represent. You should be driving the information shared when people speak of you in your absence. **You must, above all else, be clear in the values and truth you'll show to other people.** If you layer self-doubt and negative self-talk over a positive narrative, you confuse your target audience and they move along to the next candidate.

### What we tell ourselves influences what we tell others

Not only are these internal tapes creating beliefs and truths within your own hardwiring of self-perception, they also leak out into how you communicate to others. When there is an overinflated sense of importance or self-confidence, it inevitably shows up as boasting or arrogance. When there is a deep sense of inadequacy or a lack of confidence, others perceive it as uncertainty in the message delivered. Have you ever tried to buy from a salesperson who you could tell didn't believe in their own product? Maybe they avoid eye contact, hem and haw often as they sell you on their goods, and sound like they're reading from a script instead of sharing their passion for the product's usefulness. They're trying to sound convincing and confident, but you can just tell they wouldn't put that product in their own home.

As consumers of narrative, most of us are good at evaluating the truth behind the message. We can usually tell if something passes the "sniff test" by watching how the story is told—determining whether we can believe both the storyteller and the message. Once we determine how truthful the message is, we move on to evaluate the validity of the messenger. In the 1950s a popular television show launched called *To Tell the Truth*, where celebrities would try to convince show participants they were truthfully sharing an occupation, story or experience. Participants would have to evaluate not only how real or likely the story was but whether it could have actually happened to the person claiming it as truth. Watching the show, home viewers would also become fixated on trying to decipher between fact and fiction, often looking for subtle cues from the celebrities about their truthfulness or lying. When you believe what you're telling others, the likelihood they'll accept your words as truth increases, as the show confirmed.

### *What we tell others impacts what they'll tell others about us*

A powerful part of personal branding is the ability to be referred to others. When someone can introduce or recommend you by speaking about you in a way that is consistent with how you want to be perceived, opportunities abound! This drives the importance of making sure others know what you stand for, want to be known for, and your desired positioning. Being in control of how others speak of you, describe your value and promote you is when you gain control. You are now influencing the perception of you when you aren't present—online and in person. For professionals seeking to build influence in conversations, causes, clients and communities, being perceived for the skills, character traits and values you offer when you aren't in the room is powerful.

We are naturally curious beings, and when presented with truths that seem extraordinary or farfetched, we become skeptical. In a piece written for *Psychology Today*, the author notes:

> Skepticism… is a key part of critical thinking—a goal of education. The term *skeptic* is derived from the Greek *skeptikos*, meaning "to inquire" or "look around." Skeptics require additional evidence before accepting someone's claims as true. They are willing to challenge the status quo with open-minded, deep questioning of authority.[1]

Instead of leaving to chance that others will view your messages with a skeptic's mind, promote narrative that is truthful and consistent with all other personal brand attributes to become transferable. The more evidence others see of your brand consistency, the more apt they are to refer and endorse you with confidence.

Narrative, storytelling and language will surface a great deal in this book and in your career because of their importance to building reputation. Words and actions must coincide in the minds of the target audience to build credibility for the values you promote. What you say you believe in should be evidenced in what others see you do and how you make them feel. Your behaviors drive experience, and experience drives perception and brand.

## People will want to believe your narrative

In my experience studying the target audiences of many clients, when told information about the individual that may be interesting or helpful or even a bit contrary, unless there is a strong reason to debate the information or the messenger, audiences will accept what they hear or read and go about their day. The power in this concept is that giving someone erroneous or misleading information, then, could have the same impact as sending someone information that is positive and truthful. Where's the difference?

Here's an example: If you hired a new chief marketing officer who told you they were passionate about helping build the company brand, you'd likely accept it. In the first months of their hiring, you are proud to see them work well with others in the company and applaud that they bring new ideas to the leadership team. Later, if you learn that they spoke negatively about the company to peers in other companies, you might doubt the validity of the rumor, still defending your hire. However, if you later read a review this person posted on a job board where they called out shortcomings of company leadership and promoted themselves as more informed than their colleagues at the company, you might now question your decision-making skills and judgment. Initially, you'd want to trust them to confirm your own beliefs. But enough evidence to the contrary can sway your opinion. Unless there is a strong and compelling reason to question something we're told about someone who has some credibility with us, we typically accept the information. This idea aligns with the confirmation bias practice we discussed in Chapter 1 and might explain why we refuse to accept a rumor that our favorite television star committed a heinous crime, or our colleague is capable of embezzling from the company. Given this observation, the power you have to proactively drive narrative cannot be understated.

Here's another example of how the power of narrative works: Years ago, I worked with the leadership team of a global manufacturing company. Their team was internationally dispersed, but for our personal branding training they were brought together in one location. Prior to our session, my team and I deployed a perception mapping study on each of the executives. The study included a survey to each executive's colleagues, direct reports and key vendors asking several questions about their brand, communication and leadership style. For one executive, Kathy, an obvious pattern emerged: Almost everyone queried described Kathy as "black and white." They didn't use candid, direct or straightforward. They literally used "black and white" to describe Kathy. On the day of the training, each member of the leadership team was given the opportunity to briefly introduce themselves. Around the table it went, until it was Kathy's turn. She said, "I'm Kathy and I lead the R&D team. One thing you learn about me pretty quickly is that I'm very black and white. It either is or it isn't, and I call it like I see it." There you have it—Kathy used the expression so confidently and immediately that it was easy to see how she earned the reputation. This example demonstrates how powerful our narrative is in how others see us. Kathy's self-described black and white style, matched with her direct communication and leadership approach, made it easy for those around her to assign her that descriptor without much thought. It made sense, she acted that way, and there was no evidence that she was being disingenuous or misleading. Kathy was black and white.

Imagine, then, if she'd used another phrase to describe her approach. What if she'd said, "I'm Kathy and I'm terrible at making decisions...," or "I lack the judgment to hire the right people," and so on? With repetition and reinforcement, those descriptors would stick to her reputation just as black and white had done.

## Your narrative should be referable

If narrative becomes a set of keywords and phrases you direct others to attribute to you, we are reminded that when validated through action, these words and phrases become trusted and endorsed by our target audiences. Later, when those endorsements become more public, appearing as testimonials or mentions online, for example, other people begin to believe them as well. This is the power of refer-ability. Your ability to build a credible reputation is enhanced when others are so confident in your narrative and actions that they'll transfer their own credibility to endorse and refer you. This third-party credibility can pack significant weight to build and reinforce a brand.

The media also uses endorsements as testimony to your credibility and reliability. When sourcing content for a news story, for instance, a journalist may talk to several of your colleagues, former clients and employees to get their sense of who you are and how valid your side of the story is. Much like an attorney might do when calling charac-ter witnesses to the stand in your defense, others look to the words and descriptors people use about you to validate their suspicions (and confirmation bias kicks in) or dispel their fears. This is another reason why your ability to drive the narrative about who you are and what you can offer is so critical. If you aren't in front of the optics and the narrative, you relinquish control to others.

Similarly, if you send the wrong message about who you are, you also confuse your target audience. I remember working with the ex-wife of a famous professional athlete. Her former spouse was a household name in his sport, and she felt she'd lived in his shadow during and even after their marriage. She was eager to distance herself from his legacy and build her own name. But, as she pursued other ventures and as we brainstormed what she might do with her life and how she'd build her own identity, all ideas, options and possibilities inevitably brought her back to talking about her ex-husband. She constantly referred to him, repeatedly telling detailed stories of his influence in that industry, and then ending with, "but my goal remains to separate my name, business and legacy from his." How could she expect others to see her as independent from him if she repeatedly brought up his name in the conversation? The perception mapping work we did confirmed my fear and I kindly—but firmly—advised her to distance herself from his legacy by not talking about him.

### Using keywords and phrases

Keywords will emerge from your strategy work, particularly as you identify your values, evaluate where you are today and clarify your desired brand. You'll also uncover specific phrases or words that are important to your target audience, which will help them know you and feel a connection with you. The keywords that matter the most are the ones that are *authentic to your work and vision for your legacy* and are *most meaningful to your target audience*. As meaningful as you believe it will be to be perceived as a "thought leader" or "pioneer," if your target audience is looking for a "business leader" or "idea generator," they may overlook what you offer because of misdirected keywords.

As you evaluate keywords and phrases to attach to, consider how clear those are to your target audience. For instance, do people you seek to attract use those same words or would you be seen as too cryptic and miss an opportunity? Similarly, are your keywords specific enough to what you do and the focus of your work? For example, I rarely use "marketing" in my self-positioning. Instead, I rely on "personal branding" and "reputation management," because while those are more narrow and specific key phrases, the people I want to attract know, appreciate and use those words. As you deploy the tactic of narrative, remember that your goal is to align what you offer with the language of who you seek to attract.

*Consistency of narrative matters most*

As you craft a narrative to support your personal brand strategy, you will focus on being consistent across all touch points. Your narrative comes to life in many ways—from the way your company promotes you to shareholders, to the "About" section you write on your LinkedIn profile, to your biography on the company website, to how you introduce yourself in networking situations and more. Without consistency, your message comes across as fractured. In addition to ensuring that your narrative is appropriate to the platform it is on—i.e., your LinkedIn profile is focused to your online audiences, your elevator pitch is succinct and conversational, and your corporate bio on the company website is more detailed—they should all reflect the same person with the same values.

## Relationships: Building strategic networks of influencers

Whatever station you are at in your life and career, you've likely assembled a network of contacts, colleagues, acquaintances, friends, confidants, supporters, mentors and others who make up your "professional network." Separating out close friends and family, the question becomes who should and shouldn't be in your network? Who in your network helps you to influence, inspire and impact your target audience? Too often I see prominent professionals accepting every lunch meeting, each LinkedIn connection request, and having conversations with everyone at a business gathering. Their reasoning is that the more people who know them, the more opportunities they can attract. In fact, the opposite can be true. Spreading yourself too thin drains time and attention. Having too many random relationships can confuse your target audience, who might struggle to see how they fit with you. Too many people in your database can make it challenging to focus when you need a favor or referral.

Thinking strategically about relationships means asking yourself:

- How can this person help me?
- How can I help them?

- What credibility will I gain by being connected with them?
- Are there risks to my credibility by being associated with them?

This might feel like a calculated and even cold way of approaching something as emotional as relationships, but we are talking about strategic networking, not charity or social engagements. To have an effective network, you should be conscious and strategic about the people you'll build rapport with, transfer information to and from, and with whom you'll collaborate.

### Identifying strategic networking relationships

Assuming you operate within a sphere of influence (or aspire to), who you connect with matters. I'm not speaking of job title, size of investment portfolio or number of followers on Instagram. Your strategic networking contacts should be serving you directly as you promote your personal brand and build up your reputation. The four categories of strategic contacts are:

1 **Decision-makers.** As the name implies, decision-makers are ones who can write the check, approve a contract or hire, or "bless" the engagement. You, yourself, may be a decision-maker for many of the contacts in your network depending on your position, influence and credibility. An entrepreneur seeking funding would identify investors or finance and banking professionals as potential decision-makers.

2 **Influencers.** These can be people with broad and valuable networks of resources, contacts, clients, vendors, etc. They may be online influencers or business influencers or even social influencers whose name and clout carry credibility when a referral or endorsement is offered. If you're the founder of a startup consumer products company, an online influencer who shares images of your product with their followers would certainly have the influence to drive traffic to your website. Similarly, someone well respected in a community, who could publicly support or endorse you, could open many doors for your future endeavors.

3 **Information sources** are individuals with great insight, knowledge, training or skill in a specific area where you are either weak, inadequate or uninterested. The information they can share with you gives you competitive advantage when needed, and ensures you cover all bases when promoting your offer. An example of an information source could be someone who has deep understanding of social media (helpful to build up your positioning, or mitigate the damage in a crisis), accounting and finance (as an entrepreneur you might rely on your information sources until you can hire a CFO), social cues (can coach you on the best way to approach the wealthy benefactor of the foundation), and so on.

4 **Cheerleaders**. These networking contacts are critical throughout your career, not for their information or influence, or their ability to contract with you. Rather, cheerleaders are your professional support system. Every successful leader I've worked with has noted the impact and value of their cheerleaders in keeping them focused, helping them remain accountable and providing moral support when needed. Find these people and ensure they are in your network with the same focus as you would someone who can hire you.

*The role of your strategic network in advancing your reputation*

If you are a first-time parent returning to work after family leave, you might be approaching your return with hesitation, concerned that you've become disconnected from the skills, conversations and events happening at the office. Now would be a great time to lean on your cheerleaders to give you encouragement and support. Your influencers could also help pave the way back for you by including you in key events and meetings. Those information sources in your network can offer you knowledge and information on recent developments. And, the decision-makers in your career (likely your boss or client) can start to see you confident and capable, which you'll demonstrate because you feel supported, informed and validated. Starting a new company in a crowded marketplace? Why not leverage the credibility and insight of an influencer in your network who can include you in key conversations, introduce you at industry events and share their experiences from growing their own ventures?

The point of a strategic network is not to accumulate names of famous people who'll take your call. Your network should serve a specific strategic role in your professional development and growth as you build towards your reputation goals. At times, some contacts may consume a lot of your attention and at other times you'll focus on different relationships. Nurturing all networking contacts does not mean everyone is tended to with the same intensity at the same time, but everyone in your network has the potential to serve you and therefore is important to you. For this reason alone, it's vital to be selective about who is included in your strategic network, and clear on what role they will play to advance your reputation.

### How can you serve your network?

We all have that one networking contact who is always asking for something: an introduction to your chief marketing officer (CMO), your review of their résumé, an invitation to an important function your company sponsors, and so on. This contact has forgotten the cardinal rule of networking: reciprocity.

Networking is all about win/win relationships. As you cultivate networking contacts into strategic assets, you will be constantly on the lookout for an opportunity to return the favor and help them even if they don't ask. One client notes the birthdays, family vacations and book recommendations of his key contacts in a spreadsheet. When on a call with a contact, he can refer to the information he gathered earlier and the contact is impressed that he retained such details. There are many sophisticated contact management tools available to help you track your professional relationships. I recommend you use them to help manage your business and reputation.

If you forget the two-way street that is networking, if you ask more than you give, you'll risk burning out your relationships. Always seek to provide, refer, endorse, support and respond to them with what they need, as you're asking them to do for you.

## *Purging your network when necessary*

There are times we have to excuse people from our network because the relationship is no longer relevant or helpful to us. It may happen for any number of reasons: Perhaps they crossed a professional boundary or represented themselves and their values in a way that puts ours at risk, or maybe they made a bad decision. Instead of keeping people in your network because you fear hurting their feelings, remember that being careless about who you're spending time with, sharing leads with, commenting on posts online and referring to others can have significant consequences. Consider what happens when a high-profile financier is suddenly in the headlines for tax fraud and the media examines all of their relationships, colleagues and contacts. Is that the list you want to be on and defend yourself against? This happens daily in our world today.

An international client of mine experienced this the hard way. He'd been raised in a very strict Middle Eastern family, with clear values around integrity, honor and duty. He worked hard and finally found his dream career. Unfortunately, he befriended an outspoken manager who was later ostracized from the company they both worked for. Because the two were known to be friends, when the outspoken manager was fired from the company, so was my client. Company leaders perceived that because they were friends, they shared similar points of view. The fact he was fired from an employer in his industry became common knowledge and his ability to secure another career post was limited. Due to no fault of his own, his reputation was tarnished.

None of us looks forward to having to distance from someone who could be headed for a painful scenario. When you consider your own livelihood along with your ability to influence and help the contact, it might be the right decision. Had my client been in a position to advocate for his manager, or promote him and defend his reputation, things could have ended differently. Unfortunately, he did not have reputational clout to do so and got swept up in the current of guilt by association.

Another real-life scenario many senior professionals encounter is networking contacts who seek to attach to you for their benefit, but not necessarily yours. This happens when someone seeking to establish themselves as credible repeatedly "tags" or mentions you in online posts, drops your name when trying to make professional connections, and leverages your connection to them in inappropriate ways. It's not fun to be on the receiving end of this. A client of mine is a prominent figure in human resources. She connected with a jobseeker on social media, offered some words of encouragement and days later discovered that the candidate had contacted the company CEO and implied his relationship with her was much more substantial.

If this happens, I recommend assuming good intent initially. Suppose they didn't mean to undermine your success and influence by attaching to you. Presume they were ambitious and excited about the relationship with you being able to help them secure more opportunity. Assume they meant something positive instead of defensively assuming they wanted to take advantage and succeed at your expense. If or when you are shown otherwise, then evaluate the value of the relationship and decide how to act. If appropriate, have a clear and definitive conversation with them, point out that they crossed a boundary and assess their reaction. If they continue to push or overstep, that's a good indication that the relationship is not mutually beneficial.

## Digital capital: Leveraging social media to influence perception

Can you be a little bit pregnant? Can you un-see something you've seen? Can you, in fact, put the genie back in the bottle? The obvious answer to these questions is "no," yet when it comes to digital reputation, there seems to be a pervasive belief that mistakes can be erased, no one is really watching, and the online community shouldn't care. The harsh reality is that, yes, they care, and yes, they're watching constantly. What social media and the internet did for reputation management is nothing short of remarkable. When sites like LinkedIn and Facebook emerged, professionals around the world suddenly had the potential to be seen as rock stars: They airbrushed their profile photos to eliminate all wrinkles and blemishes, they hired professional copy-writers to assist them in waxing poetic about their long and illustrious careers—listing successes and accomplishments as proudly as kindergarten artwork displays on a home refrigerator—and they connected with everyone. "More friends!" everyone proclaimed as they randomly connected with strangers around the globe.

Today, hopefully, the approach is more strategic. Being thoughtful about the way you present yourself and your narrative online is crucial to building reputation and avoiding risk. When someone has a thoughtful, consistent and authentic online persona, audiences learn to trust what they see and read. On the other hand, when nothing appears online about someone, and then a negative event occurs, one side of the story takes the lead.

## Building your personal brand online

Social media and online tools have given each of us a powerful option for promoting our value and brand. The exposure your message has online, potentially reaching millions of people around the world, is mind blowing. I remember early in my business receiving a Twitter message from a marketing professional in Europe who offered to share a white paper he was curating on the idea of personal branding. He just sent it to me—a stranger—because I was building a business and needed resources. The paper, by the way, was brilliant!

Twenty-four hours a day, seven days a week, your brand is being seen, evaluated, considered and critiqued by individuals online. They are determining your seriousness, likeability, relevance to their needs and whether to connect with you. While this can make online activity now feel overwhelming and burdensome, it reveals the awesome possibilities you have at your fingertips and keyboard.

### STEP 1: CHOOSE YOUR STRATEGY AND POSITIONING

It might sound obvious that you'd start with a strategy—or, if you currently have an online presence, that you'd evaluate your strategy differently now—but many people simply jump into the deep end of the social media pool with no plan, no thought and no targets. These are typically the users of social media who find it time-consuming, unfruitful and annoying. Instead, consider social media through the lens of "how do I want my audiences to perceive me?" Your online behavior then becomes more focused and intentional and less haphazard or random. Even if you engage a professional social media assistant or firm, you should be filtering content and conversation through your desired brand, your end goal. You are less likely to mistakenly post an inappropriate cartoon or make an off-hand comment if you consider the impact of every action as it supports your desired legacy. For some, it's important to be perceived as approachable, helpful and accessible. For others, a more exclusive and reserved positioning supports their desired brand. With one client, we pursued a "Black American Express Card" model of branding—his online persona was elusive, discreet and very expensive. In person and in his work, this was how he operated: He only served very exclusive clients with high-end real estate properties in high-demand, undisclosed transactions.

Consider who you're seeking to attract and connect with online. Your target audience is likely online and they're looking for information, inspiration and content they can leverage and through which they will know you better. Are you speaking their language or using words they won't relate to or search by? The keywords, tone and language of your content should attract them to you. Are you clear on what your target audience desires to know (functional needs) and feel (emotional needs)? Does the market you want to attract need you to share information about your craft, provide inspiration during times of chaos, show them how to do something differently, or connect them to other leaders? It's your job to be very clear about your target market and what they need, so you can respond accordingly in your posts and presence online. Think of social media as a marketing tool for your brand. As a communication vehicle, your brand is expressed and communicated online to empower audiences to form beliefs and perceptions about you. Before any post, comment, share or connection, ask yourself, "How is this serving my reputation?"

## STEP 2: CHOOSE YOUR PLATFORM

Not all social media platforms are the same. Before embarking on a social strategy, consider your goal (ideal desired reputation), your strategy and positioning, and where your target audiences are active. For most of us in business, LinkedIn makes sense as it's become the primary platform for everything to do with commerce, globally. If your target consumer is on Facebook, however, consider a personal and public page on Facebook. Recognize that where LinkedIn is a business-oriented and professional site, Facebook is more social, casual and interactive. You'll find people posting about their children, holidays, political views and career struggles on Facebook. To actively engage there, your audiences will need to see a relatable, approachable and casual side of you, too.

Instagram (owned by Facebook) offers a visual platform on which to communicate. Each post must have a graphic, video or image to accompany the text. In 2018, there were 100 million active Instagram accounts. In 2020, Instagram's user numbers were rising across all demographics. Estimates are that by 2023, the number of active users will grow to 125.5 million, representing all age brackets (heaviest concentration under age 34) and geographic locations (the highest concentration being in the United States, followed by India).[2]

## STEP 3: SHARE, COLLABORATE, CELEBRATE

Social media users are expected to participate and interact with others. While "lurking" is still common, the users who are driving their brands and getting noticed are active and visible. Sharing original, repurposed or passed-along content highlights what you care about and where your interests lie. For example, if you routinely post on the topic of emerging markets and innovation, your online followers and contacts begin to see you as someone passionate and knowledgeable about new opportunities. If you're a venture capitalist, this could be great positioning for your career.

Collaborating is also important online. Simply clicking "like" on someone's thoughtful post is a nice gesture, but adding comments, insights or additional ideas is likely more meaningful. Similarly, you'll see people begin to collaborate more with you and your content. When you measure success from your online activity, decide if you're simply looking for a "thumbs up" response, or would you rather see your target audience comment, share and add their thoughts to your content?

Finally, when someone in your online network shares an accomplishment, it's your turn to congratulate and celebrate them. These gestures are meaningful to your connections, as it's often quite awkward to post, "Thank you to the Brisbane Chamber of Commerce for recognizing me as its 2021 Business Leader of the Year." But we must let others in on our successes, as uncomfortable as that is. For the person who self-congratulates to showcase their brand, reward them by publicly celebrating their success. This shows generosity and graciousness on your part, as you'll likely do the same one day, hoping to receive acknowledgment as well.

### How much should you share online?

In a 2019 article[3] I published on Entrepreneur.com, I offered advice on how much professionals need to share online to maintain reputational health and still be seen as authentic. Some of the tips I shared about what to post or not post included:

- **Be thoughtful and intentional with the comment, image, post or share before you post it.** Many missteps and mistakes occur because someone thought everyone should see the joke/meme/article and they didn't read the entire thing. There, buried inside the linked post, is something insidious, and the sender is in the hot seat for promoting it. Think through how and why this post will add value to your network and your reputation before you hit "send."

- **Consider whether someone could be hurt, upset or offended by your post or comment or share.** Calculate the risk to yourself and your personal brand if you share something that gets taken out of context, has undertones of inappropriateness or is somehow harmful to you and your reputation. If you're still willing to move forward and share the post or make the comment, you will have thought through the pros and cons of backlash and support.

- **Ask yourself: Are you potentially sacrificing privacy?** Even in this information-overloaded world we live in, we are still allowed to keep some things private. Just because you experienced it, or have an opinion about it, doesn't mean you need to share it. You make that choice.

When COVID-19 shut down business and social interaction around the world in the spring of 2020, many frustrated and upset individuals took to social media to share their anxiety, stress and fear about what was happening and when it might end. Globally, and in all languages, the social community gathered online to vent, cry and scream at their computers in communal grief. Some people even offered up their coping mechanisms, including excessive drinking and use of illegal drugs to get through the stress. As work slowly came back, and weary quarantined professionals made their way back to socially distanced workplaces, those posts remained online. In some cases, people revealed intimate personal details they later regretted. "I got caught up in the international upset and discussed the stress this pandemic was putting on my marriage, my commitment to my employer and how it threatened my sobriety," shared a colleague. She later regretted being *so* open but was hopeful that her words might have helped someone who read them. "Later," she explained, "I went back and edited those posts out. I want to remain authentic and compassionate, but there were certainly times I crossed over and used the internet as group therapy." In the long term, some of those posts could have seriously damaged her credibility and career trajectory if left unaltered. Editing out the posts later can certainly help, but who saw your comments and photos before you removed them? Whose impression of you changed after your rants? You can't un-see something seen.

## The power of Google

It's undeniable that in the twenty-first century Google has become a noun, a verb and a part of our everyday lives. Need a dry cleaner? Google it. Want to know what 4,962 plus 775,893 equals? Google knows. Curious about research into how the human brain processes data from unrelated stimuli? Google knows. We Google people, places, information, resources, referrals and even ourselves. As you embark on a personal branding strategy, a good tactic to use is periodically doing a Google search on your name, in quotation marks. What do you find? How many pages of results are returned? We call this "ego surfing" and it's a very good exercise. You want to know if anything appears about you online before someone else does. You can also set up a Google Alert on your name. A Google Alert will send you a notice when your name appears in an article, blog, post or other online forum. This can be helpful to ensure your reputation hasn't hit a snag. You can even add the name of your company to the search, or your specialty, if appropriate. If you have a common name (e.g., John Smith), it is helpful to add qualifiers, so Google sifts out irrelevant posts.

One of the most common first questions I get when someone's name has been tarnished online is, "How can we get those articles off Google?" Unfortunately, there is no way to manually or cleverly remove content from Google without taking dramatic measures. While there are companies that purport to offer this service, my clients who have engaged them have rarely experienced meaningful results. Rather than remove the undesired content, these services typically focus on tactics such as populating blogs (with the client's name) with metatags, backlinks and keywords to create activity and content that would ideally push the negative search results off to the fourth or fifth page of a Google search. For now, remember that Google is a powerful algorithm, designed to swiftly sort through massive amounts of data and return (for a search) what it deems timelier and most relevant (along with paid advertisements). To think someone can "outsmart Google" is amateur. To learn more about the algorithm, searching and data mining on Google, visit https://www.google.com/search/howsearchworks.

For our purposes, understand that once something is online and has seen the light of social media, it can't be unseen. Today, users must be mindful of text messages, photos, comments on news articles or blogs and videos, as all of these tell a story about who we are and what we value (or don't value) and impact digital capital towards reputation.

## Executive presence: Image and body language tactics of strong personal brands

Do you need a signature look to be memorable? Should you change up your wardrobe and image often to highlight different sides of your personality? The question of wardrobe and image comes up frequently with personal branding clients. Regardless of executive status and position, country of origin or reputation goals, many clients focus on how they appear to others, physically. This is a good thing because the optics of appearance and body language carry a lot of influence in the non-verbal communication of personal branding.

### What does your image say about you?

Just as your strategy and goals will be personalized to you, so should your appearance and image. I'm sure we've all seen that one emerging executive who was recently styled by a salesperson in a fashionable clothing store. They seem uncomfortable in the color and fabric of the suit. The tie seems to attract more attention than they're accustomed to and the combination of shirt and shoes screams, "I don't feel like me." As you build your image to be in alignment with your personal brand, consider that when you're clear about your brand, your audience and what's appropriate for the situation, dressing yourself and presenting a compelling image comes easy. For example, when I'm preparing to deliver a presentation to a group, I might consider these questions:

1   **How will you be presenting yourself to others?** When speaking, I consider a number of factors in deciding my wardrobe: the logistics of the event (e.g., will I be walking across a stage? Will I be on my feet for several hours? Will I wear a wireless microphone?). This helps me determine whether to wear high heels (hours on my feet? Ouch), a dress (where would I clip the wireless microphone pack?) and long sleeves (gets hot under the lights). Consider the environment you'll be in, what the nature of the meeting or event is, and how you'll be interacting with others to determine appropriateness and comfort.

2   **How do you want others to perceive you?** If I'm on stage and my goal is to garner audience participation, engagement and interaction, I'll want to present myself as trustworthy, entertaining and approachable. Dressing in a less formal, relaxed way might get me there. Or, if I'll be delivering an inspiring and forceful keynote address and need the audience to pay attention and respect my advice, I might dress in a more polished and formal manner to build seriousness in my appearance for the message to have impact. The same thinking goes to in-person meetings and video presentations.

3   **What do you want the audience to know and feel about you?** The audience you'll be interacting with should be a big part of your thought process, as you consider their needs and goals alongside your own. Even for an in-person or video meeting, consider: Do you need them to feel safe, validated, heard and appreciated? Do you want them to become intimidated and motivated to act out of fear (of not managing their reputation)?

4   **Finally, what makes you most confident and happy?** Before you scoff at this point, remember that you may have a power tie, a confidence jacket or a pair of heels that make you feel you could conquer the world. We all do. There are certain colors, patterns, fit of clothing that make us feel good about ourselves and lift our spirits. When we wear those items, we feel not only confident but authentic. We feel good in our own skin and that comes through as we project our narrative externally.

When I worked with the former COO of a publicly held company that she'd just facilitated the sale of, my client was struggling with what to do next professionally. She'd been with her previous employer her entire career, growing up the ranks to the highest level of executive influence. Before leaving her post, she'd been regularly presenting to corporate shareholders, financial media, Wall Street influencers and her team at HQ about the company, its growth and vision for the next chapter. She felt typecast by her role as "corporate executive woman." Now she was ready for a new chapter with a new focus and that meant evaluating her image as well.

She needed new photography for the website we were building for her to share her new vision and she and I discussed the setting and look for her brand. "I'm used to being photographed in a navy suit, white blouse, strand of pearls at my neck, sitting in an office behind a desk," she shared. I arranged her photography session to be in the Rocky Mountains of Colorado, which I knew she loved and where she had a home. I'd encouraged her to bring several looks for the photo shoot, as we wanted to capture different sides of her personality and brand. She brought some suits, with corresponding blouses and camisoles, as well as a few casual looks.

When I spotted the mauve/pink leather blazer, I asked her to put it on. Suddenly, her complexion had color and she giggled. It felt playful to her. We paired the look with jeans and a nice blouse and took a few photos. As she saw the reflection of herself in the camera, she remarked, "Wow, it's like I just came to life." Even today, she still uses those images on her website and in her marketing. She believes she found her look and personality in that jacket in that photo shoot as she stepped outside of who she was before.

Consider what you have in your closet right now that brings you joy and confidence. Is it a V-neck blouse that reminds you of a happy time, or a tie that was gifted to you by your staff after landing a significant client, or a brooch that belonged to your grandmother which is a great conversation starter? A colleague of mine routinely wears a brooch of a bumble bee. "People always ask me about it," she offers. And then she gets to tell how a bumble bee should not be able to fly according to physics (its wings are so small compared with the size and shape of its body), but it does. She says, "So do I. I've had a lot of hardship, but I still fly." It's become part of her signature look.

*Your body language constantly sends messages*

Countless studies on the impact of non-verbal communication agree on one thing: Much of how we take in information is through non-verbal cues. When what we see matches what we hear, our ability to accept the information rises. When we spot a disconnect, we become suspicious and skeptical.

The human face possesses nearly 30 facial muscles, which means there are literally thousands of possible expressions to be made. Micro-expressions are the fleeting, almost instantaneous facial expressions that trained experts use to detect lies, and which most of us are completely unaware we're doing. We might sense "something is off" with what someone says, but typically can't attribute it to a subtle and quick facial gesture.

Whether in person or in a virtual environment, our body language gives clues about what we're feeling. Body language includes our gestures and how we use our hands, whether we fiddle with our jewelry or hair, how we walk into a room (tall and erect or slumped over?), where our eyes land when we're speaking together, and more. These subtle or overt non-verbal cues give an indication about the truthfulness of your message, our relationship with you (today and into the future) and whether you can be trusted. Do you look someone in the eyes as you tell them they can trust you? Are you shaking your head side to side as you try to affirm you weren't present as decisions were being made? Do you turn your shoulders away from the person you're speaking to, instead of positioning yourself squarely in front of them?

Even the way you sit can tell a narrative about who you are and what you want, sometimes erroneously. I remember working with Roger, a well-respected investment strategist whose portfolio strategies earned him the nickname "The Midas Touch" because whatever he invested in seemed to succeed. Roger's biggest challenge, however, was that he had terrible rapport with female colleagues, staff and board members, and turnover among women was high in his company. We needed to work on this, as the sectors he invested in were increasingly becoming female-centric at their core.

In evaluating Roger's current brand, several issues arose, including his choice of words (he still referred to women as "girls" and occasionally called them "honey" as a gesture of affection), but more concerning was his body language. I'd been tipped off before meeting him that there could be issues. But when we sat down on opposing sides of a booth table at a restaurant for our meeting, I saw the problem. Across from me, ready for our meeting, was Roger, with his right leg up on the seat of the booth, his right arm laying comfortably on top, splayed out for me. It was a classic body language mistake. Roger's posture, while comfortable to him sitting in a wooden booth, was primal and animalistic in its nature. He seemed to be posturing to me. He appeared as the proud cheetah showing off his genitalia and vulnerable underbelly to imply he had nothing to fear and was ready. When I pointed out this observation, Roger admitted he had no idea he'd been sitting this way. We later learned he also had a habit of leaning back in his office chair, hands interlaced behind his head, chest puffed out. This was a common posture for him with males and females in the office, but the men rarely noticed. The women certainly did.

Whether it's shaking your head when giving a positive message or sitting with an aggressive posture in a meeting, your body language influences perception. Someone displaying confidence keeps their shoulders relaxed and tipped slightly back, their eye contact is forward and they offer a firm, but not too firm, handshake. Someone communicating insecurity will typically round their shoulders, keep hands clasped in front (or in their pockets) and avoid eye contact—as if they wish to disappear rather than engage. Women, in particular, struggle with common body language issues surrounding posture, handshaking and fidgeting. Many of the female clients I've coached have benefitted from having some of these counterproductive and negative body language challenges reflected back to them, so they can amend the behavior.

In a virtual setting, being mindful of your body language on video meetings can include eye contact (do you look at the camera or the monitor?), head positioning (are you tipping your head to one side, implying a submissive posture?), fidgeting or excessive movements (do you move around a lot in your swivel chair?) or facial tics (licking lips excessively, eye twitching, inappropriate smiling, etc.), which can be distracting from the message you're trying to communicate. If you suspect your body language could be sending the wrong message or isn't reinforcing how you feel, enlist the help of someone close to you. Ask for feedback on any detractors which could be coming from your posture, stance, sitting position, handshake, eye contact and the tone of your voice. Are your non-verbal cues and gestures consistent with how you desire to be perceived?

## In closing

Personal branding is a journey forward. Each of us, every day, is given the opportunity to start anew, and to begin a new path. It may not be a straight line, or an easy walk forward, but with assessment and action, you can set a course for your future that looks markedly different from where you were before. It is also a process, not an event. Building your brand into a solid and credible reputation means constantly evaluating and assessing your actions and the results you achieve. Your target audience might change, your vision of your ideal brand might mature or refine, but your values typically don't. Your values are what you believe at your core, and while they will grow with you, fundamentally who you are remains true. You'll use different words to clarify and describe your values, perhaps, but your foundation is you, and it's right. Today and always.

The tactics you'll use to build your strategy might also evolve and change. There was a time when we didn't have social media and online positioning to aid us in getting our message to target audiences around the globe. Today, we do. Tomorrow, there might be alternative ways of communicating and we'll adapt and filter which ones to pursue through the filter of where we want to end up, our legacy.

In 2020, as the world managed to work under extraordinary pandemic conditions, many personal branding tactics required shifting. No longer did we focus on the handshake, as we were mindful of social distancing, and we had to concern ourselves with building rapport and trust through the computer's eyeball on a video call instead of in person over a meal or at a meeting. We learned that working virtually also meant we had less in-person time to establish trust and credibility, to offer support and nurturing, and to connect meaningfully with peers, staff and clients. We had to find unique ways to get the attention of our stakeholders to advance our careers. For many professionals and executives who paid attention to these shifts, their brands continued to flourish. For others, the workplace proved to be increasingly challenging.

Regardless of what the global environment looks like as you read this book today, you have the ability to chart a path forward that is authentic, unique and compelling, to stand apart from others who might have almost identical résumés, and whose educational successes and professional awards mirror your own. Today, you can design your legacy and how you'll live up to it from this moment forward by designing your personal brand strategy, adding in specific tactics, and controlling the narrative about who you are, what you believe in and stand for, and how you add value to the audiences around you.

## Endnotes

**1** Price-Mitchell, M (2012) The art of positive skepticism, *Psychology Today*, https://www.psychologytoday.com/us/blog/the-moment-youth/201206/the-art-positive-skepticism (archived at https://perma.cc/NDJ3-USVE)

**2** Chen, J (2020) Important Instagram stats you need to know for 2020, *Sprout Social*, https://sproutsocial.com/insights/instagram-stats/#ig-user (archived at https://perma.cc/8T2S-W94P)

**3** Citroën, L (2019) How much do you need to share online to be considered "authentic"?, *Entrepreneur*, https://www.entrepreneur.com/article/338761 (archived at https://perma.cc/G7XS-XMKY)

# 05

# Pivoting your reputation

*When making a career or life move (e.g., from being a surgeon to an author, or from being a corporate executive to a politician), personal brands need to pivot. The work here focuses on carrying forward those reputation assets which are valuable and relevant to your next career and shedding the ones that are no longer worthy of promoting or relevant.*

Imagine waking up one day to realize that the work you've been pursuing and the career you've plotted and planned for is no longer appealing to you. Alternatively, what if you woke up to find that you could no longer continue on your existing career path because of a change in the required skills, relationships or industry. Both of these situations call for a career and reputation pivot. We make a career pivot because our job is eliminated, we decide to change directions for personal, spiritual, financial or health reasons, the demand for our services goes away, or our ability to be relevant is removed. Consider the star athlete who faces a career-ending injury, or the industry specialist who finds themselves unemployed when their industry implodes. In some cases, the change may not happen due to external factors, but rather because the individual realizes they want something different, something more, and something unrelated to what they've previously chased. All have to pivot their reputation to stay relevant. We make a reputation pivot, along with a career pivot, when we desire to take the assets of our reputation, which have served us well, with us into our new venture.

When making a career change—such as going from stay-at-home mother to working professional, or military soldier to non-profit leader, or corporate CEO to philanthropist, or professional athlete to entrepreneur—you'll want to bring forward those reputation assets that can serve you and shed the reputation aspects that no longer are needed. Knowing which assets to leverage and maximize and which ones to discard, and how to do so, is the focus of this chapter.

## Understanding a reputation pivot

### *The difference between a pivot and repair*

Many clients come to me expecting to go through a reputation repair process when what they really require is more of a reputation pivot. They believe that because their career is no longer viable, they have inherently lost credibility or value in their reputation (hence the need for repair). Reputation repair is required in dire situations in which, for example, someone is ostracized from their industry because of misconduct and where their actions may be prohibiting them from re-entering their field or re-establishing their previous credibility. As a result, reputation repair will help the individual in their efforts to choose completely different work so they can start off with more of a "clean slate" so to speak. Simply put, a reputation pivot (the topic of this chapter) is not synonymous with reputation repair. If your name is tarnished and you look to regain credibility and trust in your current market, we'll address that in Chapter 6.

In this chapter I'll share several examples of those who have pivoted professionally. Perhaps your industry is suffering, your company is closing, the demand for your skills is evaporating. Maybe you've had a change of heart and want to do work that's more personally or spiritually meaningful. There's also the possibility that other life circumstances led you to move your vision, mission and career to a new focus.

Consider these life-, career- and mission-changing scenarios that can lead to a career change and reputation repositioning:

- After a divorce, the spouse who stayed home to raise the children is suddenly needing or wanting to work. With a reputation as a parent, and maybe some previous work experience, the challenge of reinventing themselves professionally is real.

- A health crisis may provide limitations on the kind of work you're able to do. Used to traveling and speaking in front of an audience? Not as convenient when you're undergoing chemotherapy and low on energy as you battle cancer. Or, following a health crisis, career options might look different and what was viable before is suddenly absent.

- Perhaps you've become a caregiver to a family member, requiring you to work varying hours and days, and the limitations or shifts this could cause to a thriving career are noticeable, requiring an adjustment to career focus.

- A military spouse, who suddenly finds themselves putting down roots with their family in a community (where they're used to uprooting every two years), can now establish a career, instead of a string of jobs. Creating the narrative and strategy to develop a career plan is now an option.

- If the work you're currently pursuing is no longer meaningful and fulfilling and you seek more inspiring and impactful work, a pivot can happen. These are sometimes the most challenging reputation shifts, because once the individual has made up their mind that their passion is elsewhere, day-to-day operations are often frustrating and unfulfilling.

*Examples of reputation pivots*

### EVA: FROM THE BACK OF THE ROOM TO THE STAGE

When Eva came to see me, she had numerous outstanding reputation assets to her credit. She'd spent 25 years successfully working on Wall Street as an investment banker and in the 15 years afterwards, she supported a leading organization focused on advancing equality for women in the United States. Her role in the non-profit was to support the CEO and coordinate sponsors, investors, clients and speakers who ensured the organization's mission progressed.

Eva shared with me that since leaving the financial industry, she'd found her passion: Supporting and advancing issues around women's equality and rights. She was passionate about education, advocacy and furthering legislation in this area. When the organization she worked for lost significant funding and needed to close, Eva found herself curious about business ownership. Her pivot was not just from employee to owner, but it involved coming from the back of the stage to the front. People who knew her recognized her talents, strengths and passion, but as a behind-the-scenes person. "What if I'm meant to be out front now?" she asked in our first session.

My work with Eva started with categorizing and inventorying all the assets and data points from her work with the organization (those indicators of her readiness for "the stage," as we called it, and that supported her mission). We discovered that there were aspects of her reputation we needed to shed: Many in her vast network also saw Eva as support staff, not as a leader. This needed work. We focused on bringing her voice forward and leveraging her experience and passion with the new direction of her business. Through writing (blogs, articles and commentaries), speaking (small venues at first, such as local chambers of commerce, and then later big industry events where women's issues were featured and advanced) and consulting (Eva began working with large companies facilitating their diversity and inclusion mission to include programs and education around advancement of women), her reputation as an outspoken, thoughtful and passionate advocate of women's rights grew to national visibility.

### BRITTANY: SHEDDING ONE BRAND FOR ANOTHER AT THE OFFICE

When she first came to me, Brittany worried that her actions at work had dubbed her "the office mom" and were limiting her career opportunities. Brittany was hired on at the company in a leadership track: From outstanding intern to junior manager, her next move would be to a senior manager overseeing two teams, but the promotion evaded her twice. Each time, her supervisor told her she needed to demonstrate more leadership qualities and less "mom-like" behavior. Brittany had no idea what this meant. In looking at how to shift her reputation at work—something many professionals face due to their behaviors, misinterpretation of their intentions and motives, or mischaracterization of their actions—Brittany and I first had to uncover what was leading to this limiting perception (perceived as real in the minds of her colleagues) and reputation. After surveying her peers and interviewing a few managers and coworkers, we discovered:

- Brittany had undermined her credibility by withholding her opinions and thoughts during meetings. Afterwards, in hallway conversation, she might volunteer a suggestion which could have been very valuable if shared during the meeting, not afterwards.

- She was socializing with the wrong crowd. The administrative staff at Brittany's company sat in a "secretary pool" of sorts and Brittany was a frequent visitor. She felt comfortable among the men and women who were often glad to see someone from the corporate team become so friendly. However, the optics of this to senior management indicated maybe she was more at home with support staff than with the leaders.

- With a highly nurturing and caring demeanor, Brittany often brought cookies to meetings, offered to circulate the birthday card for an employee, routinely offered an empathetic shoulder for someone to cry on, or even cleaned up the conference room after celebrations. She was, in fact, assuming the role of a traditional mother figure at the office.

In unwinding this reputation, our goal was not to now portray Brittany as a cold and unfeeling company leader. In fact, we accentuated her behaviors which reinforced the warmth and compassion that made her so unique, but we also restricted her actions at work so the optics and the perception could move towards her as a high-potential leader in the company. She restricted her socializing with the support team to after hours, she resisted cleaning up the conference room and bringing cookies every Friday to the team meeting, and began publishing "office hours" in her email so her team could know when she was available for brainstorming, discussion or refining of programs. Not keeping such an accessible, open-door policy, combined with her new attitude and confidence, gained Brittany the respect for her skills, talents and contributions within the company over time and she was eventually promoted to a leadership role.

## OMAR: WHEN YOUR HOBBY BECOMES YOUR CAREER

Another example of a pivot is what Omar experienced when his long-standing career in the oil and gas industry in Saudi Arabia was challenged. Omar had worked as a project manager for each of the big industry companies, his track record was solid, but his career path forward hit a bump when, through acquisitions and mergers, he committed to work for a smaller, less known entity that was trying to make an impact in the thriving oil and gas industry in the region. This company was excited to bring Omar on board and leverage his relationships, locally and with the government. However, the company's reputation was less than stellar (Omar neglected to see the importance of this upon hiring on) and after 18 months on the job, Omar was struggling. His previous relationships were dissolving because his colleagues didn't trust his employer and he wasn't sure what to do next. When Omar first approached me, he sought to rebuild his reputation within the industry, but with another firm. He thought he needed reputation repair help.

In our conversations, Omar shared with me his passion for flying. He owned one small plane and was very proud of his flight hours and safety records. When he spoke of flying and what it meant to increase his skills there, he lit up: The smile on his face, the excitement in his voice and the passion for his craft were obvious. Omar resisted letting too many other people know of his flying passion for fear it could show he was not focused on work or was too much of a risk-taker. The more we talked about the viability of a career tied to aviation, ideas started flowing. Realizing he was in a job he hated, working alongside people he lost respect for, and worried that his good reputation could be tarnished, Omar made a bold move: He decided to focus on flying full-time. We built a strategy for him to take the positive reputation assets and relationships from his previous career and move them into this new focus. For the next year, he gave flying lessons, posted videos of himself in the cockpit before a flight explaining where they were going, shared stories of his previous work colleagues who'd now accompanied him on flights, highlighted the instruments that would be most heavily relied upon during a flight, and shared personal testimony of the experience of flying his own aircraft across long journeys. He excited other aspiring pilots into the industry and began blogging about technical aspects that worked for him and ones to avoid. Over time, Omar became a relied upon expert —others cared about his views and reviews of new aviation technologies and protocols.

Omar's following of like-minded pilots and wealthy business executives began asking him to pilot for them. Eventually, he opened a training program and a private pilot service, earning more income and enjoying more happiness than he ever had previously. He smiled more, he was a better husband and father, and found a way to set up a small organization to provide introduction to flying tools for youth who could not otherwise afford the experience.

## Managing a reputation pivot

*Part 1: Assessing your current reputation assets*

As you consider moving from one career or job or focus to another, the steps are simple, yet not easy. You'll want to carefully consider each step for its potential opportunity as well as risk.

### STEP 1: CLARIFY YOUR GOALS

In addition to wanting to do something different or doing your work in a new way, what is your personal branding goal in making this pivot? To answer that question, consider these prompts:

- Are you striving to be known for new qualities and characteristics? If so, what are they? (Write them down.)

- Have you now realized that your true purpose and mission is something else and want to dedicate your life to a new focus? If so, what was the impetus to this change?

- Are you motivated to change because the marketplace has shifted? Has the need for your work moved in a different direction? For example, the impact of the COVID-19 pandemic forced many professional speakers to find new, virtual ways to present their materials, or to leave the career field altogether.

- What other areas of your life will have to move or adjust to support this new focus? Will your family have to relocate, or your work require you to travel more, or will your spending habits need to change as you anticipate earning less?

Having clear and defined goals for your reputation—today and as you make the shift—will help you navigate the challenges to avoid and identify the opportunities to seize.

### STEP 2: LIST YOUR CURRENT ASSETS

How are you known today? Which aspects of your current reputation are working well for you and affording you the endorsements and validation you strive for? This step might require a formal appraisal (perception mapping survey, interviewing, or feedback assessment), but you can also informally poll those closest to you for information. Seek to understand the common threads of your legacy to date. What do people seek your counsel or advice on? Who considers you inspiring and impactful and why? What makes you memorable? Odds are, the answers may surprise and delight you.

Often, when you're seeking to grow, learn and pivot from one career focus to another, your current audiences support this change. You might fear you'll lose their confidence or support if you move away from what they rely on you for, but in fact, they often see your move as brave and confident, and admire you more. In Step 5 we consider your new target audience, but for this step, ask your current audience to provide guidance, insight and feedback on the assets that make you compelling and relevant.

You'll also want to inventory your tangible assets, such as:

- **How viable is your online presence?** How many followers do you have and how are they composed? If your online connections and followers are primarily in the field you're moving away from, note this. If you have a wide and vast set of connections online, pay attention to any that currently reside, or are influential, in your new area of focus. Assess and inventory your digital assets.

- **Perform a Google search on your name,** along with geographic location and industry. See what results are returned. (Note: You might also want to have a few select colleagues do this on you, too, as the results you'll often pull from Google may vary from what people who are not you will return.) Are there any negative mentions? Are the mentions from the Google search all related to your current job and industry? Are there any indicators that your move to a new focus could be problematic based on what your online reputation indicates?

- **What does your network currently look like?** Do you know people who can support, encourage, refer and endorse you in this new focus? Will you need to shed relationships that no longer serve you or could be harmful? Inventory the people you consider your true network (not just the connections you've had on LinkedIn for years). Your true network are the people who would take your call if you rang them. Categorize them according to their relevancy going forward: Who are your decision-makers, influencers, information sources and cheerleaders? Then, notate if they will be valuable in your next career focus.

- **Do your image and marketing need to be revised?** For example, if you'll be moving from a C-suite corporate banking position into a volunteer position working with children in third-world countries, you'll likely need to project a different and more appropriate look and image. Consider the environment of the opportunities you're moving towards and determine how much of what you currently have to work with (from wardrobe to photos of you and published written copy describing you) will need to shift and change.

## STEP 3: DECIDE WHICH ASSETS ARE MOST VALUABLE TO
## TAKE WITH YOU INTO YOUR NEXT CAREER

For this step, you may need to do some broader research. It's important to understand and study the reputations of leaders or successful individuals in your new area of focus. You won't copy them, but you'll learn valuable insights about their success, ability to build relationships and establish credibility.

When my client, Jennifer, left her corporate career in software sales to start an online blog and e-commerce site, she was fortunate to know several leaders in the space who'd established credibility as advocates for women in tech and who'd gone on to build large and visible platforms for their brand and message. These individuals were important contacts for Jennifer as she sought to pivot from sales professional to blogger and influencer, passionate about advancing roles for girls and women in technology. But Jennifer lacked insight into the other components of her pivot. She was unclear about what her audience needed to know and feel in order to see her as credible. What she needed was a solid understanding of where the global movement to attract women into technology jobs was headed. To learn about her new focus, Jennifer became a researcher and student: She quickly amassed online resources and contacts who were vital in helping her chart a strategy to reach this new audience. She formed relationships with girls and women who were interested in careers in technology but didn't know where to start. She began speaking and teaching at industry conferences, on university campuses and on popular podcasts to better immerse herself into her new field and learn where the pain points were.

She realized it wasn't enough to have a great list of contacts or to have thousands of online connections. Jennifer learned that her new focus would require her to earn her way up to legitimacy. Even after a long and successful career in technology on the sales side, she lacked the credibility to establish herself as an authority as a tech entrepreneur and advocate. Once she committed to forming viable and sustainable relationships, and contributing her expertise and insight with others, she was able to begin to pivot her reputation across to the new focus.

STEP 4: IDENTIFY GAPS BETWEEN WHERE YOU
ARE AND WHERE YOU WANT TO BE

Similar to the process of initiating or building your personal brand, now's the time to identify any gaps in reputation assets that need to be created before you make the pivot. Will you need to establish subject-matter expertise at the outset of your new venture? Or, is that something that will be developed over time? How far are you today (current reputation and brand) from your goal?

With insight about the distance between where you are (current brand) and where you want to be (desired reputation), begin to plot out how you'll achieve your goal. For example, if you're transitioning from a role as a stay-at-home parent to that of a business professional, consider:

- How up to date are your skills and training? If you'll need to upskill or reskill to compete more effectively, add that timing into your strategy.

- What adjustments to your life and lifestyle will you need to make to ready yourself for the shift? Will you need daycare support, emergency contingencies and backup plans that are unnecessary in your current role?

- Are you financially, spiritually, emotionally and physically ready to make the move or do you need more time to prepare and plan? Have you discussed your plans with your family and support system, on whom you'll be relying for encouragement and help?

- Have you considered any and all stakeholders whom you currently have relationships with and whom you wish to retain? Have you built a strategy to inform them of your pivot and then nurture the relationship forward?

- Are you fully invested in the shift or still evaluating options? Note: Neither is a right or wrong response. If you are actually still considering options, you'll want to lengthen the timeline of your move to accommodate additional research, consideration and planning.

STEP 5: UNDERSTAND YOUR NEW TARGET AUDIENCE

When changing careers, your target audience often changes as well. It's likely that you'll need to build relationships with completely new targets. As you imagine yourself in your new role, who are the individuals in positions to support, endorse, refer and advocate for you? Who will you now serve? In discussing the building of your personal brand, consider the needs and wants of this new target audience. What do they need to know about you to consider finding you credible? What do they need to feel about you to consider engaging in a professional relationship with you?

As a huge football fan, I was thrilled when a retired NFL player reached out to me for assistance in building his personal brand after leaving the league. While he knew the ins and outs of football, he now found himself working in financial advising and wanted help bringing his valuable assets and name recognition forward into this new space. We spent a great deal of time assessing and inventorying the assets he had to work with. In his football career, he was known for his ability to consider the moves before executing a play and his supportive and encouraging attitude towards others on the team. He was known in the community for his philanthropy and support of local charities, as well as his approachable nature when fans greeted him out in public.

While the technical aspects of running football plays down field would not prove valuable as a financial advisor, his reputation as someone who was considerate, trustworthy, supportive and generous was definitely valuable! In the weeks leading up to his career change, we studied the local clients he'd want to target. Our research showed that these people cared about trust (first and most importantly) and long-term relationships with their advisors. Track record of performance was also important, but my client wouldn't have this, starting out. Since he'd be working through a local advisory firm that had a stellar reputation for intimate and careful client services, he focused on leveraging the company's brand as well as delivering on the promise of his own brand as he learned more about the people he'd now serve.

*Part 2: Creating the strategy to pivot*

Your strategy will be as broad and comprehensive, or as nimble and swift, as it needs to be. Resist the urge to over-construct and over-judge at this point. If the option to pivot is immediate and your assessment reveals you are capable and poised for success, don't hesitate because you believe it should be harder or more complicated. I've worked with many professionals who tangled up their plans in over-analysis and over-preparation only to later discover that the window of opportunity had closed. If you're ready and confident, make the move.

At the same time, it's acceptable to take your time if you still feel uncertain or unprepared. Once you've made the emotional commitment to change your career, it may feel like you need to move fast for fear of changing your mind or learning something that would make the move a poor choice. Sometimes this is the exact reason to go slower. Ask yourself if you've truly considered the change and impact to your lifestyle, family, career path and future. Do you feel pressured to change because friends and family are encouraging you? Are you truly qualified to establish your brand and reputation in this new area or do you have reputation repair work to do first? When you've thoroughly considered options and conducted your assessment and are confident about this move, then build the strategy.

STEP 1: DEVELOP A GO-FORWARD PLAN

Using the goal or goals you identified in your assessment, consider where you want to end up. What is your ideal situation? With that end goal in mind, you can begin outlining what you will do first, second, last. You'll consider when you will communicate your change to your employer, colleagues, investors and board of directors. Add in how you plan to manage pushback, questions or concerns from colleagues, competitors or the media.

The timing of your transition should also be part of your strategy and plan. Do you anticipate a long lead time (for instance, you're leaving the military and have 18 months to plan your next career) or a short one (if, for instance, the work you're doing today is no longer viable and you're taking advantage of the situation to change your career focus)? Inventory those assets which you can leverage for the long-play strategy (institutional relationships, brand equity as a subject-matter expert, educational credits which are unique and valuable, e.g., a PhD in Human Factors could be interesting as you move from being a UX/UI lead designer to a psychologist studying depression). The long-play assets can slowly and subtly migrate over to positioning in your new career. The assets that aren't as unique or valuable (for example, your network of professional contacts if you're completely changing career focus) may need to be shed gradually. Consider how the timing could work in your favor, which assets are more neutral in their value to you, and which are irrelevant or even potentially negative.

Your plan directs how you'll begin the transition and pivot, what benchmarks and roadblocks you can anticipate hitting, and what success will look like. Be as specific as you need to be to feel confident and clear about your direction and goals and avoid being so specific that you create unnecessary rigidity. Plans change, processes morph, strategies evolve: Ensure your plan has enough flexibility and movement in it to accommodate unexpected challenges as well as opportunities.

Consider enlisting the help of an accountability partner or coach to assist you with crafting and executing your plan. This person may be one of your supporters or advocates, or you may hire a consultant. Once your plan is developed and you feel comfortable with the direction and allocation of resources needed to pivot your reputation, engage a partner. A word of caution in soliciting external feedback here: Unless they are skilled at navigating this level of career counseling, avoid allowing others to unduly influence your strategy and plan. You know yourself well. You have clarity of vision and mission. While it's helpful to get outside perspective and input, by the time you're writing your go-forward plan, you've done your due diligence. Stand firm in your conviction and avoid the temptation to believe someone else knows what's best for you.

## STEP 2: CRAFT YOUR NEW NARRATIVE

When I coach an executive who's facing a major career pivot, a common question I hear is, "How can anyone else understand why I've made this change?" The answer is usually, "They might not, and that's why you have to spell it out for them." As you prepare to move your career, network, work, focus, passion and leadership skills to a new venture or area, you should decide how to tell the story—or narrative—about the move. Will you say you lost your job and were forced to find a new path? Or, will you highlight the aspects of your career and reputation to date that have perfectly and elegantly meshed to lead you in the direction of your new mission?

As I was readying my brand for entrepreneurship and founding a company under my name, I looked back on a 20-year career in corporate America and struggled with the reality that the optics of my career path could paint me as someone who was unfocused and non-committal. I'd changed jobs many, many times. Typically, after about 2.5 years in a position, where I was often hired to fulfill ambitious goals and objectives, I'd achieve success and move on. I had been successful in each job, hitting objectives and meeting goals, but then the idea of continuing on the path, or implementing the grand strategy I'd launched or replicating the sales success I'd achieved left me uninspired. So, I'd change, sometimes moving to a completely unrelated industry because to me that was the most challenging and exciting. Can I replicate success again? Which strategies and systems can I design that will show achievement in this new, unfamiliar environment? I did this over and over for many years. Someone looking at my résumé would likely be impressed with the successes, achievements, results and awards, but might question my loyalty to my employer or my ability to stay focused. Admittedly, it certainly crossed my mind once or twice!

Instead, I looked back and realized I needed to craft the narrative that told the story of why I'd moved so many times. Now, as I pivoted from corporate executive to business owner, I realized I thrive on strategy, challenge and designing measurable systems to help companies and people position themselves for success. This was my gift. In launching my own company, I promoted this narrative confidently and consistently, and added that I'd been in so many industries that I was very well versed in many dimensions of business from many angles. I was able to craft my own narrative about my background and what it meant going forward. Without me telling the story of what my career meant to date, why it all qualified me to be an expert consultant, speaker and writer, the marketplace could have easily interpreted my background unfavorably and made my future uncertain.

Your pivot to a new focus or venture or career may not be obvious to those around you. It is your job to ensure they see the logic, rationale and reasoning behind your move and that comes from your narrative. You must control the "why" before you can explain the "what."

### STEP 3: IDENTIFY THE RESOURCES YOU'LL NEED

As you identify your new focus or mission, and inventory and assess your current assets, you may realize you lack certain skills, qualifications or relationships to help you succeed. You may need to factor in time to learn new skills or earn credentials. If the career you're moving towards requires more training or expertise, can you learn this alongside your current work? Will you need to completely step out of the workforce and pursue learning full-time? Are the skills or training you need to learn achievable on the job? Consider whether any gaps exist before you make the transition. I've seen too many instances where an executive feels they are qualified to do a different role only to learn later that their competition is highly trained and credentialed, making them more competitive.

Similarly, ask yourself whether you have the right relationships and networking contacts to support, endorse and refer you. If you'll be pivoting from one industry to another, would it benefit you to become familiar with key influencers in the new industry, form relationships with decision-makers and information sources who can smooth your transition?

Consider what resources, if any, you are missing and think strategically about how to attain them and when you'll need them in place.

Ideally, do this before you actually depart your current workplace for this new career.

## Part 3: Building reputation in your new career

When Richard first contacted me for help, he boldly stated, "I've realized my life's work is unfulfilling, I've identified what I want to do with my career, and I'm worried that if I tell other people they'll think I'm nuts and lose faith in me." Richard was facing a career pivot. As a successful and well-respected venture capitalist in the digital media space, Richard was highly credited with a unique ability to pick and invest in ventures that grew fast and fierce. Almost every company in his portfolio had been acquired by one of the large media companies, at a handsome profit of course. Richard knew how to make money. Lots of money.

During a family vacation to remote parts of Africa, something sparked inside him. While on the trip, he and his family explored areas that were off the beaten path, talked to indigenous locals who were committed to improving the area's limited access to things like clean water, electricity and other vital resources. He heard firsthand from passionate advocates who were concerned about the sustainability of the environment and a two-week vacation turned into a life-changing event for Richard. When he returned to the United States, he'd made the decision to commit his talents, connections and skills to solving these important global environmental problems. He decided to use his investment and finance acumen to ensure the viability of the planet by influencing triple-bottom-line investing— showing how the social, environmental and financial levers could combine to create important global value. This was quite a departure from investing in, and spinning up, tech companies for sure!

Richard told me he felt like he was starting over in his career. He spent many months figuring out the key "players" in his new industry, understanding the science behind climate change, global social levers and sustainability from the macro and micro views. We intentionally avoided promoting him as a subject-matter expert and leader right away, even though his learning and understanding of the concerns and opportunities grew quickly. Instead, as Richard attended conferences that brought together the most innovative and well-respected leaders, he listened more than he spoke. He read the journals, adding his comments and observations to online articles where he could confidently share knowledge, observations and insights. Over time, he recognized familiar faces at the conferences and followed up with meetings and lunches to continue conversations. As more people were let in on his plans to move his career and reputation focus, Richard's online activity (primarily LinkedIn and his blog) became ideal for sharing his view on the industry and beginning to more visibly promote his thinking and insights. Richard knew there was no rush to be in the spotlight. That time would come. He often reminded himself that he couldn't move too fast or his investors for his current fund might question his attention and commitment to their investments.

As Richard did, you may naturally find additional areas of your past that you may need to shed as you build reputation in your new focus. Some of the relationships from your past career no longer will serve you or could actually harm your reputation going forward. Richard spent less time in conversations around technology innovations as he focused more on sustainability ventures. Naturally, several of his investment colleagues lost interest in hearing of his new passion and those relationships grew cold.

Building your reputation in your new area of focus should reward you with new relationships, opportunities to contribute and lead, and knowledge. You'll find yourself stretched and challenged in real ways (your commitment to this new direction may be resisted by some who question your motives), yet the rewards you'll achieve can validate your decision daily. One of my clients left a lucrative, seven-figure corporate job to work with inner city youth, and while the income was dramatically different, they told me, "I've never felt more personally and spiritually wealthy in my life." Resist the naysayers and doubters and remain focused on the goal—to contribute, lead and create impact in the way most meaningful to you.

## Fending off imposter syndrome

As you navigate this new direction, imposter syndrome may casually creep in. Many of my clients tell me they are all "gung-ho" and as they work the strategy and plan we develop, self-doubt creeps in and they question, "Who am I to do this?" "Why do I think I could be good at this when those other people have spent years doing this work?" Imposter syndrome is a well-known phenomenon in this context. When you begin to doubt yourself, your right to have what you've earned, and your ability to contribute in authentic and meaningful ways, you might suffer from imposter syndrome. In reputation-building, imposter syndrome is particularly harmful. When we previously discussed the importance of narrative, the first step was self-talk: what you tell yourself. Self-talk influences what you tell others, which ultimately impacts what others tell others about you. If you approach your new reputation focus with doubt, hesitancy or a belief you will be called out as fake, those feelings can easily leak into how you project and communicate your value to others. The impact could be a loss of credibility, erosion of trust, and reputation crisis.

If feelings of doubt creep in, or imposter syndrome shows up for you, resist the temptation to stop your progress. It's normal to evaluate your choices when faced with stressors that are uncomfortable and unfamiliar, but your strategy should reassure you that you've done the due diligence, you've crafted a plan and you're working the steps. The prize at the end is work and reputation that are personally and professionally rewarding and meaningful.

## In closing

Whether you design your career and reputation pivot and have dreamed of it for years, or you wake up one morning and realize you were destined for something different, transitioning your reputation assets from one path to a different one takes finesse, skill and planning. Here, we've looked at the steps to take to move the parts of your reputation that make you valuable and credible into your new area of focus. Even if the change is coming because of circumstances outside of your control or liking, you retain the ability to move through them and towards a mission and vision that give you gratification, personally and professionally.

By taking inventory of the qualities, characteristics, exposure and relationships you've earned and built to this point, sifting out the ones that will not serve you going forward and capitalizing on the ones that will, you can establish a solid reputation for the qualities you desire as you pivot to a new focus. Remember, your audience might still want to learn who you are, what you value and what you can offer, but streamlining your messaging, positioning and online capital will ensure your reputation with your new target audience is built on a foundation of trust and authenticity.

In the event you are pivoting your career and reputation because of a crisis or negative event, next we'll look at ways to repair reputation using strategies and tactics designed to help you get your name back.

# 06

# Repairing your reputation

*Reputation repair is needed in the challenging situations when you have made a misstep or misjudgment, or you simply were caught "in the wrong place at the wrong time" and your credibility and career viability are in jeopardy. This chapter walks through steps of assessing the situation and distilling the crisis down into action steps, and provides guidance on repairing a tarnished reputation to ensure career viability.*

When I launched my consulting business, I was initially hesitant to offer reputation repair counsel. I imagined I'd be working with insensitive and ruthless individuals who'd been careless, defiant or whose moral code was vastly different from my own. I feared being seen as a PR "fixer" for politicians, business leaders and wayward celebrities who'd want me to clean their reputation after an ill-worded Tweet received backlash, an inappropriate photo was emailed to all staff or a career misstep fueled venom from online mobs. Instead, I learned that many people in many industries, countries, jobs and cultures suffer reputation crisis, sometimes not even from their doing and very often from simple ignorance or carelessness.

In 2018 I authored an article about reputation repair after working with several clients whose career had been torpedoed as a result of workplace bullying. The response to the article shocked me! School teachers, journalists, business professionals, social media influencers, students, professional athletes, moms, dads and others contacted me to say the same thing had happened to them. They had been bullied, gaslighted, picked on or tormented at work and the public ridicule and rumors cost them their job, confidence, reputation and in some cases their careers.

In this chapter, we'll look at reputation crisis and repair from several angles. Using real-world examples, we'll examine what to do if your name is attacked or tarnished, how to assess the damage and design a strategy to fix the situation, and how to decide when to make drastic changes and when to come clean and take accountability. Reputation repair is not easy, fast or painless. Regardless of whether you are the victim or the unintentional or intentional perpetrator, the impact can be similar. Negative information will follow you mercilessly unless you take action early and swiftly to manage how the narrative plays out.

## Understanding reputation damage

Do you remember the story of Richard Jewell, the security guard working the festival at the 1996 Summer Olympics in Centennial Park in Atlanta? He was wrongly accused of planting a bomb which he discovered, and which later detonated, injuring many festival participants and killing three. His story was most noteworthy because of the tremendous damage done to his name, career, family and personal confidence when he was publicly and legally pursued as the main suspect, even though he was later proven to be innocent. Some described what happened to Jewell as being "tried in the media" because popular opinion and rumor created widespread belief he was, in fact, guilty of a crime he didn't commit.

Reputation damage happens when your name, image, body of work, career and other artifacts of your brand are tarnished dramatically. We see this happen online, in person and across industries. Reputation damage can impact your ability to secure future work, pursue opportunities, and threaten your ability to form valuable personal and professional relationships. When someone asks about you, looks you up online, or is confronted with the story about who you are and what you did, they may conclude you are not worthy of further consideration. Previously, and in part due to social media, when we thought of reputation damage, we imagined companies or industries suffering after corporate missteps or improprieties. Today, individuals are suffering financial loss, career challenges and personal devastation to their relationships and health following reputation damage.

Reputation damage also occurs when beliefs and expectations about who you are fall short. For example, we expect doctors to be good listeners and act with empathy. When they are crass and indifferent to our needs, their reputation can be damaged. Similarly, when we expect politicians to represent the needs of our community and learn later that they took bribes from special interest groups, our trust is shattered. Even rumor or suspicion of brand damage can have devastating consequences.

Reputation damage also results from negative reviews about you and your work, unflattering media coverage, accidental sharing of confidential information, or accusations from people who've worked with you. Even the accusation can cause reputation damage. When faced with a negative comment or review about you or your work to a company review site (e.g., Glassdoor), resist the temptation to fight back with all your might. The online community often watches to see how and where the subject of the criticism will respond when called out online. A client of mine faced a situation where several former employees took to review sites online to post erroneous and inflammatory comments about him as the chief executive officer (CEO) of the firm. They alleged misconduct ranging from financial to sexual. They sent links to their comments to investors, the trade media and other stakeholders in an attempt to get the CEO fired. Because they'd shared specific information that only certain employees would have been privy to, my client was able to engage law enforcement and legal resources to put an end to the harassment and slander before it went too far. Even as far as it got caused damage, but it was reparable. My client was tempted to start posting positive responses on those same sites—using an alias—but I advised him against trying to defend himself (anonymously or otherwise) on a platform as unregulated and uncontrollable as social media.

Best practices in crisis management say that you don't fight a battle online. Take it offline and evaluate your options before posting a response. If you inflame the online community, you might make the situation worse; if your actions are seen as "guilty," you make the situation worse for yourself. Either way, it's a tough scenario. In some cases, however, a response online is appropriate. If you're able to think through options and conclude that an apology is warranted (e.g., "I'm sorry you were disappointed with my hair styling services. Perhaps we could discuss how I could earn back your trust?"), tread lightly. Some people take to the online community in the hopes of garnering freebies or perks as incentives to quiet down. That can be akin to blackmail and not a way for your reputation to flourish. Others watching the online exchange can see it as an opportunity to partake and now you have a bigger problem on your hands.

More and more, social media provides the ideal platform for jilted lovers, disgruntled employees, and jealous or fearful competitors to lash out against who you are, what you stand for and what you offer. Without any substantiating evidence, they can post online, often anonymously. I remember being contacted by a woman in Italy whose reputation was being sullied in the media. While I didn't end up working with her, to this day her story stays with me. She'd run a successful textile company for many years and traveled often for work. On one trip, she met a man and they began a relationship. She believed him to be divorced yet learned later he was very much married. She ended the relationship soon after, but his wife had found out about the affair. His wife made it her personal mission to destroy the business owner's name and company. She set up fake social media accounts in the woman's name, complete with her photo (grabbed off the internet) and personal information. She posted lewd and horrible images and messages. The wife also created websites and blogs designed to discredit the business owner and shared erroneous information on the sites. Numerous attempts to contact the web hosts were unsuccessful and the Italian woman was told that it was possible the wife used a multi-hop router, so each time she connected to the hosting company's server, it used a different internet protocol

(IP) from a different country, making the actual geographic location undetectable.

I later heard that the Italian woman had pursued legal action against her ex-lover in order to stop his wife from these attacks, yet there were no available remedies technologically or legally otherwise. As shocking as that is to believe, this is the world we live in.

*What can lead to a reputation crisis?*

There are many reasons someone ends up in a reputation crisis, including:

- believing you are above reproach and taking liberties in sharing your views and opinions, learning later that there are consequences to being outspoken;
- a photo, blog, comment or relationship from your past is discovered later and deemed incongruous with your current positioning or social thinking;
- carelessly sharing, posting or commenting on something online that results in a misperception of your values and brand;
- feeling entitled and thereby participating in illegal activities and misconduct, which gets filmed or noted and shared publicly;
- through your actions and communication, earning a reputation as an inappropriate or hostile boss, colleague or leader, making it a challenge to establish your reputation otherwise;
- being in the wrong place at the wrong time—photographed at an event with a (later) convicted criminal or otherwise unsavory individual; working for a company where a leader is convicted of a heinous crime and those around them are implicated as being complicit;
- becoming a victim of workplace bullying, leading to a tarnished reputation and a stigma that follows you from job to job;
- someone in your family posts something offensive or outlandish online and you're conflicted between supporting them and distancing yourself.

A reputation crisis can also result from feeling unempowered and unable to stand up for yourself or advocate for your needs. I've worked with several clients in this category. Whether or not they were advised by counsel to refrain from defending their position, they missed the early signs something bad was coming. Believing that the negative press would "blow over," they refrained from taking control over their narrative and situation.

### Distinguishing between corporate and personal reputation damage

Many of you reading this book are the face of your company, firm or even product. Your character, lifestyle and positioning have become synonymous with what you sell or promote. When the product or company is involved in a reputation crisis and your name is attached, you are affected as well. Consider the CEO who takes personal responsibility when their airline faces headlines because of incidents on their planes. To observers it can seem that the CEO is responsible for the reputation of the company, and vice versa.

When you are in the active role as spokesperson, figurehead or public representative of a company or organization, inevitably your reputation is directly tied up with both positive and negative events. Even so, there are ways to elegantly and subtly separate your brand (without sounding alarms or breaking rules) from the company's brand if you see a train wreck coming. For example, if the company is poised for a hostile takeover and your goal is not to continue with the new venture if offered, it may be wise to begin creating brand assets elsewhere, so you can retrieve and develop them later. You might become active on a new social media platform and post images of your life, hobbies and aspirations that do not conflict directly with your current role. This can help your audiences learn more about you and give you a platform to launch from when you're ready to make a change. Or you may start writing a book. While you're still focused on your current work, craft a book that speaks to your next venture, passion or focus. When you've made the move, you will be in a better position to polish up the book and enlist a publisher than if you started from scratch later.

Public figures who represent a cause, issue, company or product often find themselves tangled up when challenges to that cause, etc. arise. There's a transfer of credibility when you say you believe enough about the cause to get behind it. When the cause is later exposed to be a fraud, or not viable, your credibility can also be impacted. For this reason, and others, one should be very choosy about the public-facing issues and organizations you attach your name to.

## The impact of social media on reputation

Prior to the onset of social media, when someone had something positive or negative to say about a client, colleague, their boss or a politician, they'd share that insight over the fence to a neighbor, with family at dinner time or maybe even write an "op ed" to the local newspaper. The ability to spread that insight far and wide was limited by other people's desire to participate in the distribution of the initial feedback. If you didn't like a restaurant, you told your friends and maybe they told their friends. Today, a single stroke of the keyboard can drive great attention, interest and concern towards a business, cause or individual. Today, anyone with access to the internet has the power to begin, participate in or fuel conversation, negatively or positively.

## Example of social media's reach

### THE METOO MOVEMENT

While the phrase originated more than ten years prior, in 2017, when a celebrity tweeted about sexual abuse at the hands of famed Hollywood mogul, Harvey Weinstein, and called upon others to declare they'd also been abused, the MeToo movement began.[1] Celebrities, business professionals, athletes, executives, students and others came forward to publicly declare their status as a survivor of sexual assault, misconduct or inappropriate behavior. In many cases, perpetrators were publicly shamed and prosecuted. High-powered leaders, public officials, business professionals and celebrities in Hollywood, corporate America and on Wall Street found themselves accused of abusing their power and status by assaulting and behaving inappropriately around women. Prominent individuals were fired, and advocacy in support of victims of sexual abuse grew substantially.[2] Survivors felt supported by those who posted their own experiences, and high-profile men (and women) worried they could become potential targets for inquiry and examination of their behavior as this movement grew in the media. Several clients I worked with at the time said they felt as if the lens of scrutiny was turned on anyone in a position of influence over another (i.e., manager, leader, boss, etc.).

For many of my clients, this became a game-changing situation. They prided themselves on being respectful and inclusive of women and other diverse populations, yet suddenly found themselves questioned by their human resources teams or boards of directors to ensure nothing could be brought up against them. They were defending themselves, and preparing for a defense, against a crime they didn't commit. Very unfamiliar territory, indeed.

In some cases, my clients' colleagues, business associates, attorneys, financial advisors and investors were publicly accused, causing my client to become concerned the accusations could transfer to them (guilt by association). While this movement certainly empowered and advanced the voice of victims, the MeToo movement also highlighted how public scrutiny can impact the careers, reputations and livelihoods of individuals and how challenging it can be to remedy or get ahead of speculation and news given the quick nature of social media. Scandals in the past seemed more contained to an industry or company, but this one crossed all industry boundaries.

## MOB OR HERD MENTALITY

Online, the anonymity users can feel by creating social media accounts under fictitious names, using stolen or stock imagery for avatars and then posting content is powerful. Someone may feel inadequate or powerless in their "real" life, yet they can quickly incite a crowd to join them in sharing outrageous and blasphemous content online. Mob, crowd or herd mentality is a term often used to describe behavior driven by emotional, rather than logical or analytical, basis. Since the nineteenth century, researchers and psychologists have studied what happens when seemingly unrelated people come together and appear united and committed to advancing the same idea or cause. This behavior can be used for good as in the case of a quick and massive fundraising effort designed to support a family in need after a tragedy or a corporate whistleblower who steps up to announce company wrongdoings. However, it can also lead to behavior that will require reputation repair for the subject of the attack. One person who posts their outrage over the behavior of a company or individual and claims they have information to support their claims can be joined by others who jump in and support and advance an idea, cause or notion they may not fully understand, have basis for or find rational.

In a reputation repair situation, it's important to determine first if this is a random mob attack, or if concerned former employees, clients or other stakeholders do, in fact, have reason to be concerned and have the information needed to support their position. With a mob scenario—people coming together to pile on an idea—controlling the narrative looks different. In the spirit of this chapter, "mob events" will describe the negative behavior of members of the online community who often anonymously take an idea, rumor, comment, suspicion or action and run with it, giving it perceived legitimacy through the sheer number of online users who appear to support and advance the notion. In this situation, there may be a rational reason for holding back initially and evaluating whether the idea or thesis gains traction. If this tactic is adopted, a plan should always address mitigating risk and exposure if the event does, or does not, take off. Refraining from engaging with the mob, refuting their claims and defending yourself takes tremendous discipline and restraint! It's been known to happen, however, that the mob turns in on itself, and members of the group begin to defend the victim and advocate for truth. This is a best-case outcome indeed.

### GASLIGHTING

Gaslighting, on the other hand, is where a perpetrator manipulates the confidence and self-esteem of a victim or recipient, causing them to question themselves, their beliefs and their sense of what they know because of the other person's actions. This form of psychological manipulation can begin small, with subtle hints of inconsistencies or missing pieces, driving the subject to question their perspective, competency and sanity. Later, the subject of the attack may experience devastatingly low self-esteem, self-reliance and rational thinking, anxiety and depression, even feelings of hopelessness, leading them to make poor choices and question their future. The person doing the gaslighting may be motivated by a desire to bully the person they perceive as weaker, may seek revenge because of a past wrong, or could be curious how significant their efforts could become by belittling and confusing the subject.

Gaslighting has huge potential to impact and harm reputation. Without realizing it, many victims of gaslighting begin to retreat and feel insecure and helpless as their confidence erodes. They resist contributing to important conversations, pursuing career opportunities, being active on social media or sharing their fears and concerns with others. They might even lash out publicly in ways normally uncharacteristic of them, but out of desperation to change the situation they're experiencing. This, in turn, can fuel the perpetrator, leading to even further career, emotional and reputation damage. I have worked with clients who come to me in this shape: they are downtrodden, sad and sometimes hopeless. In these cases, my counsel typically includes engaging with a trained psychotherapist who can help them heal as well.

If you're reading this chapter because you face a reputation crisis, ask yourself where the situation initiated. You may have been a victim of gaslighting without even realizing it. Did you do something to start the cascade of events leading to where you are now? Or, did someone (or others) instigate negative pressure and attention on you, leading you to react in a less-than-ideal manner? Looking back on what got you into the position you're in now, were others helping to craft that situation? Is it possible you were manipulated or coerced into believing a certain way and then acting accordingly? If this is the case, consider whether others were also on the receiving end of this treatment, and whether their support might be helpful to you as you proceed through the repair process. Understanding what led to the decisions you made and the situation you find yourself in is critical to understanding what you have the power to change or modify going forward.

When I first met Peter, an experienced software architect, he seemed confident and hopeful about his future and goals. He expressed ideas about starting his own company one day, leveraging the many years of work he'd done with several of the big technology companies in the Silicon Valley community, even though he was not from the area. After our first coaching session, however, the façade cracked: Peter quickly dove into self-doubt, reluctance, uncertainty and a lack of excitement about what he could do as a business owner. He hedged every idea we discussed with statements of, "but I'd never succeed at that" and "what makes me think I'd be good at leading others?" and so on. A few well-placed questions to Peter revealed that he'd been the victim of gaslighting in his life and career—from a father who questioned his career path and undermined his dreams, telling him he'd never succeed in business and insisting he stay working on the family farm in Nebraska, to his first boss who ridiculed his systems and code (later stealing those assets for his own use). Peter portrayed confidence at first, but it was purely superficial. Underneath, he was filled with self-doubt, a lack of confidence and a hopeless view on what he was capable of. Building up Peter's confidence, credibility and positive reputation assets was hard work, for both of us. We focused on mindfulness work, surrounding him with positive people and situations to rebuild his confidence. He spent more time volunteering to serve others, received expert psychological counseling, and committed every day to being the person he knew he was, not the one he'd been cultivated to accept. His boss, I'd later learned, had continued the gaslighting of Peter long after he left the company, routinely sending him texts and emails undermining his work and reminding him that he wasn't capable of what he professed to want to pursue. But now, Peter felt empowered to dismiss the messages from those who didn't have his best interests in mind and forge his career forward.

Working with Peter was emotionally taxing for both of us, but the resulting career he found made it worth it! Peter found the confidence and positioning to launch his software company and later sold it for a handsome sum, enabling him to pursue more passions of his.

## GOOGLE: CRAWLING, INDEXING AND THE ALGORITHM

We can't minimize the impact of Google on reputation management. Most of us "Google" someone's name prior to a business meeting, job interview or date. We routinely search for images, articles, news or information through the massive and efficient search engine as we consider what we can learn (know) or decide to feel about the person we're querying. Today, Google has taken a prominent role in building, managing and repairing reputation.

When I receive an inquiry from someone needing help repairing their reputation, inevitably they ask, "How can I get that bad stuff off Google?" We know that because of the power of information at our fingertips, and the likelihood that users won't dig too deeply into what they find online, we believe most searchers will take what they find on the first few pages of a Google query as evidence. Google describes its search functionality this way: "In a fraction of a second, Google's Search algorithms sort through hundreds of billions of webpages in our Search index to find the most relevant, useful results for what you're looking for."[3] Their published information shares that the Google algorithm searches constantly, evaluates relevancy, location, usability of sites, etc., to return responses. As new information is posted, "crawlers" find it, index it and determine its importance and relevance to users searching for that content. All of this work happens quickly and often.

What this means for you is that when Google finds something it determines to be important, such as a news article which mentions your name, user behavior impacts how that information is catalogued. If someone searching your name clicks on the first link that shows up in the search, Google's algorithm interprets that as validation that the link is directly relevant to what people are looking for.

While this is an overly simplistic explanation of what happens, it's important to note that if you repeatedly search for yourself and click the links to articles that speak negatively about you, you may be helping the algorithm verify that the article should be prominent on Google's search for your name.

I'll refrain from offering you a deep and complex technical lesson on how search works for three reasons: first, negative search engine optimization (SEO) and search algorithms are constantly changing and evolving. Second, most of what you need to do does not involve getting into back-end algorithms and trying to influence search to an SEO expert's level—and finally, because much of it is over my head as well. The clients I work with understand that to repair their reputation and manage negative information found online, you don't "remove something from Google" or "manipulate the algorithm" or "trick the search feature" as some reputation and SEO professionals might advertise. Instead, understand what's on Google, work to reduce its importance and significance by posting valuable and targeted content that is more directly related to who you are, ensure your relationships and other positioning efforts are aligned with your values, what you stand for and what you can offer, and in essence "push" information down in the search results by creating positive, real and authentic content instead. We'll discuss this more below.

## How to repair your reputation

### When the "issue" isn't your doing

Today, many people find themselves in the cross-hairs of a reputation crisis through no fault of their own and are truly innocent of any wrongdoing. Whether the victim of a reputation attack or simply being in the wrong place at the wrong time, the number of cases of negative reputation is staggering. Here are three real examples from clients I've worked with.

MICHAEL

Michael was a long-time, well-known children's author under long-term contract with a large publishing company for his books, cartoons and animated videos aimed at an audience of children aged 5–10 years old. His stories were rich with positive lessons, love and childhood experiences that parents enjoyed sharing with their children. Michael's publisher was preparing for a high-profile publicity tour in 12 months and media attention was growing around his forthcoming collection of books.

When he called me, however, I could hear desperation in his voice, "They're trying to ruin me!" he almost shouted into the phone. "They've taken over my reputation online and are destroying my credibility." Michael's website had been abruptly hacked and replaced with a pornography website. A search for "images" on Google under Michael's name returned graphic sexual images. He was clearly the target of an online attack, as parents looking him up prior to the launch of his new children's book series would indeed be concerned by what the internet searches revealed.

This was not an easy fix. After assessing options, our first steps included pulling Michael's website offline for a while (terrible timing as the publisher was ramping up his visibility). We brought in web experts to install new firewalls and deterrents to prevent his current URL from being redirected to malicious sites, acquired numerous new URLs to redirect all entries to a new website for him and began the process of removing images from search results, too. I will admit that even the most seasoned experts I have in my database were stumped by the sophistication of the tagging and location of the images posted under his name on Google. They were almost untraceable—as servers pinged all over Europe, Asia and beyond—and therefore hard to remove. In this case, at the time we were able to involve Google directly in removing the information, which was doable but not easy. Google prides itself on the purity of its powerful search engine but is not also seeking to have anyone misrepresented. Here, they were very helpful and the information was removed.

FRANK

Next was my client Frank, who experienced levels of workplace mobbing and bullying unlike anything I could imagine. A well-loved, season-record-holding men's basketball coach, Frank's career and confidence were destroyed by false accusations during his coaching career at a local college. Some less-than-ideal players were unhappy with being "benched" and complained to college administrators about Frank's favoritism for other players. These disgruntled players, along with their parents, who'd paid good money to have their sons participate in collegiate sports, alleged that Frank's coaching style was in fact "antagonistic, preferential and inappropriate." Frank endured an internal investigation, was sent to "charm school" for anger management and ultimately cleared twice by college adminis-tration, who reassured him that if he stayed quiet they would support him and his reputation would be cleared. Meanwhile, a local college newspaper reporter began an online campaign to discredit the beloved coach online.

After two years of negative press in the college paper, workplace bullying by colleagues and feeling undermined by his coaching staff, who sought to protect their own reputations and isolate him, he resigned. When I met Frank, he was heartbroken at having to leave a vocation he cherished and sought a way back. After all, he'd done nothing to deserve this. In addition to suffering emotionally, Frank now suffered a fractured brand online. When someone Googled his name, the results all pointed to the unfavorable media attention around his tenure at the college. The proposed strategy I created to help Frank rebuild his name and career involved many levers, start-ing with re-establishing his positive outlook, confidence and reputation. First, we tackled his inner personal critic before setting out to deal with the external public perception. Second, I focused on his online reputation repair on social media. Frank needed more information about him and by him online, and not just a blog full of SEO keyword tags, as had been suggested to him elsewhere. Frank needed to be more public about who he was, what he valued and why coaching was his passion. He needed to highlight his successes, his collaboration with student athletes and their parents, the many years of volunteer coaching he offered to young basketball players in inner city leagues, and his vision for his career going forward to show strength, resilience and confidence. Together, these approaches helped Frank see how he could rebuild his future and reclaim his reputation.

We talked about his desire to remain in coaching and mentoring, and his passion for inspiring young men. Frank and I had several fairly emotional coaching sessions in which he worked on separating fact from gossip—reminding himself that he had done nothing wrong and working through his regret at not resisting when the administration instructed him to keep quiet. Next, we worked on repairing his name on Google and on social media. When the college blog's news about him became known, Frank removed all other online assets: He had removed his LinkedIn profile and other social media accounts. Online, Frank had no presence except the negative articles. Because he wanted to work with young people, he and I set up an Instagram account where he could share more of his hobbies and interests, and post family photos, including those of his three sons. Instagram, we assessed, was where Frank's targeted age group participated. Using a carefully crafted approach, we started building an online presence. He resurrected and retooled his LinkedIn profile to more effectively communicate his true values of servant leadership and the mentoring of young men and athletes. He began blogging, reposting like-minded leaders and creating his personal messages about leadership, resiliency and sportsmanship. Students and parents who had revered him as a coach and professionals who were inspired by his message began reaching out to him. As Frank's efforts pushed down the negative online search results, he continued to explore, articulate and galvanize his personal values, which ignited his spirit and love of coaching.

Eventually, Frank returned to coaching at another school with a very values-driven culture. If questioned by students or parents about the college newspaper reports found online, Frank calmly and confidently gave his rehearsed response and their concerns were quickly dispelled. Today, Frank continues to blog about topics around leadership, mentorship and coaching, and continues to use Instagram to build his brand, share his successes and promote others. He now stands tall and proud and his team are breaking records in their division!

## FREDERICK

In another example, Frederick contacted me after a two-year hiatus from his career. Previously, he'd been a well-respected and well-known business leader in his country. He'd launched and built many successful companies, served on non-profit boards, and received numerous awards for his leadership in the commercial real estate industry. When he came to me, however, Frederick had stepped away from his philanthropy and career because of a very public firing he'd received from the board of directors of his last company. As he explained it to me, prior to the global market downturn of 2008/09, companies like his were anticipating high growth for the future. He'd made significant acquisition recommendations to his board and they were excited at the prospects. As financial markets plunged, however, his board put the brakes on any expansion or growth plans. Instead, the company that Frederick started and grew to viability was facing a tough economic future. Outside investors and the financial media paid close attention to his moves. Suddenly, Frederick found himself in the spotlight, and not in a good way. His strategies were being questioned. His growth plans were examined, questioned and challenged for their validity given the economic uncertainty. When the board of directors decided to pivot the company's course in a new, more volatile direction and that move proved financially devastating, they publicly announced that the move had been Frederick's idea and he was soon terminated because of such poor guidance and leadership.

At the time, he tried to assert his position and announce his innocence, but the markets were in turmoil and no one listened. The idea that he wouldn't have spearheaded the move, or at least fully supported it, seemed far-fetched, so most followers, investors and journalists believed the story of his poor guidance. In response, a few months after leaving the company, Frederick relocated his family to a more rural part of the country, where they could recover and he could decide what to do next.

When I met Frederick, our first step in understanding what had happened was a deep intake session. Frederick and I looked at:

- where he'd missed early warning signs that he didn't have his board's support or endorsement;

- where he might have identified advocates and foes earlier in the process;

- the impact on his reputation—an assessment of media write-ups, op eds and bloggers focused on the impact of the company's fall was easy to accumulate;

- anecdotal feedback he'd received about what was happening that fell into his blind spot;

- an inventory and catalog of his past supporters, influencers and advocates who remained loyal to him;

- why he'd felt powerless to defend his position and assert his innocence.

We also looked at the assets that had made him successful multiple times before this incident:

- Frederick had a vast network of contacts in financial circles, government agencies, among private business professionals and social entrepreneurs and philanthropists. As things began crumbling and his termination was announced publicly, there were many individuals who rallied around him, offering support, encouragement, introductions and ideas for what to do next. While this was a real asset, because Frederick abandoned his network when he moved he would need to rebuild the relationships.

- His business track record was well documented and publicized by the media and followers. He'd been mentioned in numerous articles and case studies of entrepreneurism, business strategy and even for his leadership during the good and bad times of business growth. He'd even spoken on the topic of entrepreneurism and business strategy at local colleges and universities.

- Frederick was a consummate learner. He read multiple books each month—on business, personal growth, self-actualization, societal shifts and global concerns. He was well schooled on current trends and happenings in his industry and others. His thirst for knowledge and learning, I believe, was what led him to me as he realized he needed assistance in turning his reputation around.

The strategy we designed for Frederick was a long play. Since his eventual goal was to re-enter the business community, we sought to re-establish his credibility and the value of his leadership within smaller organizations and governmental agencies in his new community, in order to subtly transfer those back to his previous community later. In his country, the government was held in high esteem, and working with the government held a cache of credibility and prestige. Our strategy empowered Frederick to feel in control over his world again, and he received praise and accolades from staff and local leaders about the difference he was making.

Simultaneously, we established multiple online assets for Frederick as a consultant and freelance advisor to businesses either in his industry or looking to join the complex real estate field. We published well-written and potent blogs, articles and videos of him presenting his ideas to local groups of both experienced professionals and students. He formed relationships with influencers in the government and soon received a contract to do influential and important consulting work on a high-profile new development. This led to a full-time position within local government, where he further established his credibility and talent and eventually took back the good that his name had been attached to. Today, if you searched for him by his full name and country, you would find links to his current work, accolades and awards, and much farther down in the search you can find outdated news articles of his previous involvement with the company that fired him.

## When the issue is your fault

We'd all undoubtedly like to believe we are beyond reproach and would never make a mistake or take a chance that could land us in a tenuous spot, publicly. At least that's what many of my clients who've found themselves in a reputation crisis thought initially. Take, for instance, Juan. As a tenured poetry professor with a well-known East Coast university, Juan made a huge mistake: He formed a consensual romantic relationship with a graduate student, violating Title IX rules. Title IX is a well-recognized statute protecting students from being discriminated against, harassed, targeted and/or denied participation in any educational program solely based on sex. Teachers, professors and coaches are trained and coached on compliance and rules around Title IX and the consequences of infractions. The university Juan worked for over many years reminded him that Title IX clearly states professors and their students should not engage in romantic or sexual relationships. Yet, he did.

When I met Juan, he had been through the Title IX investigation and disciplinary process, had lost his marriage and custody of his young sons, and was no longer in contact with the student with whom he'd had the affair. Headlines in local and academic press had reported extensively on his case, making his termination from the university an example for others in academia to remember. Juan had lost his family, his career and his income. What now? He was an internationally known poet, often giving guest lectures and readings on university campuses around the world. He considered many options going forward, but the three that we evaluated most closely were:

1 He could change profession completely and pursue a different career path, outside of literature, academia and his community. This option was less ideal because his sons lived nearby with their mother and Juan was hoping for a shared custody arrangement in the future.

2 He could remain in the community and try to stay employed in the literary world. He considered working in a bookstore or offering tutoring to young writers. He worried, however, that he'd be constantly reminded of his mistake by community members he'd encounter.

3 He could launch an online consulting practice to publish materials and guidebooks and coach aspiring poets on publishing and promoting their works. This option gave him the most comfort—

and seemed the most financially lucrative—as it was less likely to put him face to face with judgmental critics.

Over the next few months, Juan built a respectable website, began blogging and vlogging (video blogs) about his craft (poetry) and sharing his posts on social media. He sat down with various community members over coffee to discuss what had transpired, took full accountability for his transgressions, and told them he looked forward to opportunities to regain their trust as a member of the community. This strategy proved highly successful as slowly he was being referred local writers to mentor, he was invited to speak on his body of work at regional writers' symposiums, and over time, his online consulting business grew. He developed workshops and held them in beautiful locations all around his hometown. A Google search of Juan's name still showed the headlines of his public mistake and punishment, but it now also included links to his website and blogs, articles about his new programs and work, and even video testimonials from his current and past students speaking about his impact on their careers.

In repairing his reputation, Juan and I worked on a long-term solution. Given that he'd lost his income, my initial fear was that he'd want to fix things fast. Instead, he comprehended the gravity of his mistake and that it was going to take a lot of work to earn back the trust of those around him. Juan understood what his indiscretion cost him—personally, financially and professionally—and never passed blame or hinted at an excuse. "I messed up," he stated when taking full accountability for what happened at the time and afterwards. This, I believe, also helped him regain credibility within his community, both locally and in academia.

While frustrated about the lack of options he perceived in front of him, Juan was also clear about the assets we inventoried:

- He had credibility for his work. We looked at what had earned him credibility in the past and whether those things were replicable in this new situation. While his behavior and judgment were questioned, his work had lasting and meaningful impact. We could leverage this credibility to rebuild trust in Juan.

- There was possibly more external validation to gather. Was there the potential for third-party credibility from influencers in the literary field, academia or his community? This uncovered tremendous opportunity as some of his greatest public supporters were quite influential and their public endorsements, support and references carried a lot of weight.

- Juan maintained a healthy and positive outlook. While he may have wallowed at home, or vented and complained to me, publicly he kept a positive, confident and hopeful demeanor when speaking to his network, his new students and his clients. Attitude, we know, is important and Juan always projected strength, humility and confidence (not arrogance or sadness), which made it easier for others around him to believe things would be okay for him.

Ultimately, the combination of personal accountability, targeted networking, moving slowly and intentionally, and leveraging the reputation assets he maintained enabled Juan to create a new career path for himself. At times the pace felt slow, other times he felt under a microscope. Through it all, he didn't waver from the narrative we'd crafted, which shone a light on his authenticity and humanness, communicated his passion for sharing the gifts of literature and poetry with others, and showed his unwavering commitment to earning trust again in the minds of those he sought to influence and impact.

*Steps to assessing and repairing the situation when you're in reputation crisis*

As we've learned with Frank, Frederick and Juan's situations, reputation crisis can impact one's family life, career and livelihood in the present and going forward. Quick action is needed to understand what's happened and take inventory of available options, but a knee-jerk response is typically not the wisest choice. Instead, a long-play solution, building on what has worked for you in the past and assessing how current circumstances are influencing the options you're presented with, is advisable. Regardless of whether the situation you're facing is of your own doing or not, there are critical steps to take to assess, understand and plan to repair your reputation.

## STEP 1: ASSESS THE DAMAGE

What has really happened here? Are your reputation and livelihood in jeopardy or did someone insult you and hurt your feelings? It's natural to get upset when someone online attacks you, your company or your mission, but are they damaging your reputation or just trolling for people to annoy online? Separate out what's happened, the short-term and long-term implications and impact, and what you have the control to fix or remedy as a first step.

Ask yourself if there's truth to what is unfolding. Is someone spreading rumors about you and your abilities? Do you have enough public testimony and endorsement to offset this hurtful gossip? Did you lose your cool with a peer in front of the company and someone filmed it? Has the video gone viral or can you talk to the individual about deleting it? As best you can, evaluate what has happened, what potentially can come from it, and what impact (positive or negative) it can have on your career and reputation.

## STEP 2: DON'T IGNORE THE SITUATION

Pretending no one saw what you did, the articles aren't online, your boss doesn't know about it, or your investors will never find out doesn't work. One person finds out, and then everyone knows. Particularly if the negative information is widely available through Google or social media, ignoring it can make it worse. One client fought me on this point, arguing, "If I don't play, I can't lose," but that isn't how reputation works. If you ignore it, we believe the side of the story that's getting featured online.

Ignoring the situation can give others the time to create and build a narrative that works against you. While your strategy may include holding back for a bit, always be prepared to respond. Consider whether it makes more sense to control the narrative at the outset. Do you need to confront the person accusing you, should you apologize for your behavior at the beginning or should you let your online audiences rally and defend you? Regardless of whether your strategy directs you to get ahead of the information publicly, or you're taking a "wait and see" approach, have a strategic plan for managing the situation and mitigating risk.

### STEP 3: RESIST TAKING DOWN ALL OF YOUR SOCIAL MEDIA ACCOUNTS

In response to negative press online, many people's first response is to vanish from the online world. Disappearing doesn't always help. Yes, you can remove the comment features from your blog and posts, but vanishing can hurt more than it helps. Your strategy for working through the situation will dictate how, when and where to remove yourself online, but remember that by doing this you're removing any possibility someone learns a contrary view to what they've seen that's unflattering or hurtful.

For example, a professional accused of acting inappropriately with coworkers might determine that removing their Facebook profile makes sense to maintain their privacy. After all, that platform is social and playful in nature, possibly reinforcing a casual and reckless lifestyle on behalf of the professional. They could, then, keep their LinkedIn profile to show their professionalism and commitment to various community organizations. Removing all social media and disappearing might imply there's something to hide.

### STEP 4: SEPARATE EMOTION FROM FACT

This is a hard one for most people. When someone attacks you online, fires you from a leadership position, accuses you of something you didn't do, or calls you out on a mistake you made, it's hard not to take it personally and get emotional. Unfortunately, this is exactly what they hope will happen, and which often does. When you get emotional about the situation, you might react spontaneously, erratically and defensively, which means you are not acting with intention and clarity. Instead, surround yourself with a team—this can be close friends, family, consultants and advisors—who will help you maintain perspective, keep you calm and advise you on the options presenting themselves. These people should also be asked to help you separate out emotion from what you're experiencing.

In a course I created on LinkedIn Learning called "Repairing Your Reputation," I offered this advice:

> You don't want to fire back an email or a Facebook post or march down to someone's office until you've had time to assess the damage and the impact and gotten a hold of your emotions. Ask yourself, is this a case of hurt feelings or has my actual reputation been damaged?[4]

Often, how you respond and react to the incident is as revealing (confirming or dispelling) as the validity of the claims.

### STEP 5: SET GOALS AND CREATE ACTION STEPS

Fashion a plan to articulate where you are now, where you want to be and how you'll get there. For example, if you're a medical doctor who is being brought up in front of the boards because of misconduct with a patient, and news has gotten out to your community, your goal might appear to be, "Get this bad publicity off Google," but in fact it's more realistic to say, "Regain trust and credibility with my patients and the medical community." Set a clear goal and then chart the steps you'll need to implement to achieve that goal. Your plan might include:

a   What do I need to own and take accountability for?

b   What can I refrain from mentioning or discussing?

c   Who do I need to apologize to?

d   Will I need to attend training to ensure I don't repeat the behavior? Can I communicate this once I'm finished?

e   Which relationships do I need to mend first? Second? What barriers exist to repairing them?

f   If I'm able to continue my practice, how will I communicate and behave to show that I've changed my ways?

g   How will I respond—now and in the future—if someone brings up my past mistakes?

h   When will I know I'm past the mistake and feel comfortable and confident in my work?

Recognize that your goal may not be the same as those of the people around you. Your colleagues, family and supporters might have their own goals for the relationship you'll have with them going forward.

### STEP 6: UNDERSTAND WHAT YOU HAVE CONTROL OVER

As we discussed in Chapter 1, we cannot physically control another person and therefore cannot force them to trust us, believe us or work with us. However, we can influence, inspire, inform and impact them, which can lead to a behavior or belief we desire them to have. If someone finds you to be arrogant and standoffish, then acting in a more approachable, inclusive and welcoming way can work to convince them otherwise.

We also know that online there are limitations. Carelessly posting something offensive, hurtful or inappropriate and then deleting it doesn't necessarily remove the photo or comment. There are followers—even software applications—that scour the internet and look for indiscretions or missteps and then publicize them. While you removed the post, it can remain as a screenshot. If it's online, it may be permanent.

Context, however, gives us more control. When you have easily accessible information posted about who you are, what you care about, your skills and expertise, and then something negative is posted, it's easier for the reader to put the negative headline into context. Was this indicative of a pattern or was this an isolated mistake? Is this their true character or an oversight? When you establish trust and there is context to reinforce your belief, then something negative is sometimes written off by viewers.

### STEP 7: ASSESS WHETHER OR NOT TO TAKE LEGAL ACTION

It's natural to want to retaliate and take legal action against someone who is saying negative things about you, whether true or not, to other people and online. Before you file a lawsuit, become familiar with the differences between slander, defamation and libel, and retain legal counsel for advice. These actions can be time-consuming, costly and at times more public than the initial comment or post.

Even with legal advice to pursue action, consider the long play scenario: You file a defamation suit, the other party makes the move public and claims outrage, you fight it out in court and in front of the media, and if it does get resolved in your favor, who posts that and will the public announcement outweigh the negative attention? This should be considered from legal, financial and professional perspectives. Unfortunately, in some cases where a legitimate claim presents, it's not worth the cost or personal and professional sacrifice to seek legal victory.

## STEP 8: MANAGE YOUR RESPONSE IN A PUBLIC SETTING

Should you proactively take the issue to the public, try to get in front of an impending headline and control the narrative? What happens if you wait and let the story play out? Is there a possibility your online audiences would rally and defend you, giving you a brand lift without you having to get involved? When the situation is potentially high profile, expert counsel and advice may be warranted. As the individual at the center of the conflict or controversy, your perspective is likely skewed by how you perceive the variables. A trained and experienced brand or public relations specialist can advise you on options, timing, consequences and platforms on which to go public, if that's the best course to take.

Regardless of whether you have the choice to get ahead of breaking news or not, when online chatter turns hostile, resist fighting your battle online. This can feel torturous if your name is being discredited, your work is being ridiculed, or your family, company, community, team, etc., are being discounted and criticized. Remind yourself that often the posts online are coming from "trolls"—people who spend their time posting anonymously, hiding behind a keyboard with a sense of entitlement and superiority because you can't confront them in person. These individuals often strive to gaslight or inflame others, causing the recipient to lose their composure, and the trolls then continue the banter until they decide to move on and leave your reputation shattered. You aren't fighting a viable opponent, and they have little to lose by getting you enraged enough to make a critical and public mistake.

### STEP 9: CONSIDER BRINGING IN REINFORCEMENTS

As mentioned above, there are times when bringing in advisors is helpful and productive. Consulting with legal counsel, crisis management professionals, personal branding and reputation management experts, and public relations professionals can help you work through a reputation crisis. Interview them personally (avoid letting others do the screening for you—this is *your* career and name) and be sure you feel comfortable and confident in their skills, experience, understanding of your situation and ability to provide solutions and support going forward. This is not the time to feel intimidated by the individuals or team that will help you through this.

Public relations firms, crisis management agents and reputation management experts help their clients avoid, thwart and defend against reputation crisis. When possible, identifying early indicators of a threat enable them to help the client get ahead of the story before it becomes well known, sometimes even changing the direction of the news. In this instance, the client is advised to decide whether to confront the story before it's published (thus taking the shock value out of the news piece), to ignore it, or to build a case to discredit or refute the story, if it's untrue. If it's factual, the client has the resources to form a narrative to explain their side of the story, create a defense and show reparations (how they'll make sure it never happens again).

### STEP 10: MEASURE IMPACT AND RESULTS

How will you know when you've repaired your name and reputation? What indicators are there to show you're moving in the right direction with your restoration efforts? While some of the impact and results you'll see are tangible, some are quite anecdotal. For instance, you may see more positive results appear from a Google search of your name. You might be invited to apply for leadership positions, regain entry into circles of influence you were previously outcast from, or notice that no one brings up your past mistake when meeting you for the first time. Similarly, you may feel more confident and in control over how you would handle it if someone inquires about a headline they read. You should begin to feel more selective and careful about how you communicate your value, thereby ensuring that your target audience sees you've made a change, are focused on regaining their trust and moving forward.

Unless it is a specific part of your strategy, refrain from introducing what happened or bringing up the past—particularly if you feel compelled to "get it out on the table before they bring it up," as is often tempting. Your goals and strategy will include milestones to look for and assess. Measure those and celebrate success whenever you can. If you find yourself in a backslide, and the negative information is gaining traction again, review your plan, regroup with your support team and start again. Depending on the severity of the infraction, you might need to take a few runs at it before the people who depend on you, who were impacted by what happened and who need to trust you do so again.

## When reputation is beyond repair

In fact, there are times when all the steps outlined here are not sufficient to help someone regain credibility, re-establish their name and brand, and continue on the same career path. I remember meeting with a female doctor who was at the center of a firestorm not only because of the kind of medical services she performed (legally), but because of the organization she worked for. Her employer was in a heated, very public, battle over funding, and the media and social media voices began to target her as a figurehead for the services she performed and the organization she represented. She was truly in the cross-hairs of a reputation nightmare. When we spoke, she told me she and her family had received multiple credible death threats and had "gone underground" to a remote and secure location. I couldn't even have her phone number or email for fear our communication could be traced to her. She'd explored several options to regain her name and credibility, including changing her name on her medical license and even leaving the country. Later, I found out she had, in fact, relocated her family to another country, changed her name and was living in the hopes that she could one day not fear for her life. This is obviously an extreme option for an extreme situation.

There have been many cases of high-profile targets moving to small towns, changing their names and appearances and trying to re-establish themselves in a new persona to escape a negative past. With the onset of social media and the proliferation of personal recording devices (everyone has a cell phone with a camera, it seems), this is getting harder.

## In closing

I believe we're all capable of making mistakes, yet some are more public than others. When that happens, or if your reputation is attacked through no fault of your own, reputation repair strategies are warranted. Getting your name back, re-earning and re-establishing trust and credibility, and improving your reputation online is not a quick fix. It's a timely and sometimes very emotional process.

I've worked with many clients who've been financially, emotionally and spiritually drained from a reputation crisis. In some cases, their families and support system stay intact, in others they don't (adding to the financial and emotional toll). For each, however, there is a way forward. For some it means taking a few steps back and redesigning their skills and career path, and for others it is being able to maintain their livelihood, albeit in a new city or community. I've worked with a medical doctor who left medicine after an affair with a patient and moved into a successful career in pharmaceutical sales. I've helped an executive who poked fun at investors on an "open mic," was fired and went on to become an inspirational high school teacher and blogger. I've even worked with highly decorated military officers, fired and demoted from their position over misconduct, who went on to build successful careers in real estate, digital marketing or even motivational speaking.

There's no telling which mistake, misstep or situation can plummet someone into a reputation crisis. What may have been tolerated or acceptable yesterday suddenly seems grounds for termination and public ostracizing. For many of the clients I've helped, situations felt random, abstract and "out of the blue." The impact of the MeToo movement or a mob rally cry on social media has swept up individuals who either were unaware that their actions crossed a line, knew it but ignored it, or were mistaken for someone else. In my experience, to regain credibility, strategy and thought should be applied quickly and early to put the client in a position of responding, not reacting, to what's coming at them.

## Endnotes

**1** Gill, G and Rahman-Jones, I (2020) Me Too founder Tarana Burke: movement is not over, BBC, https://www.bbc.com/news/newsbeat-53269751#:~:text= Tarana%20began%20using%20the%20phrase,Harvey%20Weinstein%20 of%20sexual%20assault (archived at https://perma.cc/AJ7Q-P2EQ)

**2** Carlsen, A et al (2018) #MeToo brought down 201 powerful men. Nearly half of their replacements are women, *The New York Times*, https://www.nytimes.com/ interactive/2018/10/23/us/metoo-replacements.html (archived at https://perma.cc/ 8AQ7-3LEY)

**3** https://www.google.com/search/howsearchworks/ (archived at https://perma.cc/ A56M-87QH)

**4** https://www.linkedin.com/learning/repairing-your-reputation/assess-the-damage- and-impact?u=2125562 (archived at https://perma.cc/F6MC-CWLJ)

# 07

# Agree to stay the course

*Here, you'll make a personal commitment to reputation-building. This chapter highlights the choices that you'll face and the decision-making criteria that your reputation strategy gives you, and it will empower you to stay focused on your desired brand goal.*

You've likely noticed that the process and steps I've outlined so far are simple, but not easy. Building, deploying and maintaining a personal brand strategy takes attention, introspection, market evaluation and discipline to be effective. As opportunities present themselves to you, you'll inevitably find yourself tested and even tempted to make choices that may not be aligned with your desired brand. Maybe you'll consider working with an investor who has a questionable track record; perhaps you'll be tempted into accepting a job at a company whose values don't align with your own; or possibly you'll be asked to represent yourself in a way that feels inauthentic in order to advance your career. Brands are made stronger when challenged, but recognizing when you are being seduced away from your goals is critical. Often, temptations will disguise themselves as great opportunities—you might even find your support network cheering you on—but when your best judgment and your brand strategy tell you it's not a good option, you'll need to stand firm in that commitment.

In this chapter, we'll look more closely at how to make the agreement with yourself to uphold your brand in the face of temptations or when you're at a crossroads. We'll examine some ways you might find yourself tested, and how to course-correct if you give in to temptation. Remember, your brand is your value proposition and it reflects who you are and what you believe in. Making the commitment to yourself to live up to the standards and values you've set, to achieve your desired brand and legacy, is a powerful move requiring confidence and clarity.

## Creating your personal brand agreement

### Why you'll need an agreement

It was a little over a year into my new business when my brand and goals were tested. As a new business owner, I was sourcing work, interviewing for client opportunities, networking with influencers in my field and promoting myself heavily online. I knew I'd focus more intently on personal branding, yet I still worked some in the corporate sector as I transitioned my company into only personal branding services. One pitch I pursued taught me a lot about the agreements I needed to make to stay the course of my vision. It happened in 2009 when the financial markets were still in turmoil, making new work hard to come by. Understandably, then, when I was told I would soon be awarded a large branding consulting contract for a local business, all of my supporters were elated. This was great news! The income from this project would cover several mortgage payments, plus some. My husband insisted we go out to a nice restaurant to celebrate!

But after deliberating, I had to deliver the bad news to him and the others: I was going to turn the opportunity down. Stunned, my husband and colleagues couldn't believe me, so I explained: As I set out to build my brand and earn a reputation personally and professionally, there were many markers and values I was hanging everything on. I was crystal clear about what those were and the desired legacy I was working towards. Upon close examination of this opportunity, there was misalignment on three fronts between what I stood for and what this opportunity afforded. First, the people I'd been interacting with at the client's office were not pleasant or nice. They truly expressed a disdain for the project they were mandated by their board of directors to complete: a rebranding of the company. They perceived this work as a "necessary evil," they said, laughing at what must have been hysterical inside jokes. It might sound petty, but I dreaded meeting with them and felt insignificant during our conversations. The second reason I was going to pass on the opportunity was because while I was confident I would do a great job (the work was something I'd done a hundred times previously and was completely in my wheelhouse), they would be inclined to want to refer me to others. Who do we tend to hang out with? People like us! And, if they aren't nice people, they'd likely refer me to other not-nice people, which was not what I was looking for. And finally, I recognized that the scope of this project meant I'd have to pass up any other opportunities that arose for several months. It would be that much work. Was I really willing to give up hope that all my positioning and marketing efforts were leading to better clients than this? No.

I remember the conversation with the client when I told her I respectfully needed to pass on the opportunity. "Do you realize how bad the economy is right now? These types of jobs don't come around often," she said. I know I panicked for a split second. Had I made a mistake? Would I regret being steadfast in my commitment to my reputation and the goals I'd set for myself and my business? No. It stung at first to turn down such a profitable project, but soon afterwards (literally within days!) my phone started ringing and the emails began coming in from prospects I'd been nurturing for months. They were ready to get to work with me, they wanted to learn more about my services, or they wanted to explore collaborations. All of this goodness and abundance came in from my ability to agree—and stay committed to—my value and the legacy I was pursuing, without compromise.

Does this feel far-fetched to you? I've shared this belief and story many times with clients, mentees and audiences. Then, later, I get the follow-up emails: "I did what you said! I stayed true to my values, didn't compromise on what I stand for and how I can add value, and the work/clients/job/relationship showed up!" Yes, it really does happen. Personal branding requires more discipline, commitment and agreement with yourself than you might believe you are worthy of receiving. But when you do, you are rewarded with what you deserve. If you'll do the hard work, if you'll make the hard choices and use your brand as a filter to evaluate, and stay consistent with how you show up, you will be rewarded with opportunity.

*Your brand as your central operating system*

Many of my clients are in the technology sector, and one mentioned to me that my description of a personal brand working as a filter, or set of criteria, was actually the description of an operating system. "All other features, systems and applications feed and build off of the operating system," he explained. "If the operating system is incomplete, fractured or flawed, the other parts and pieces won't work correctly." While I think he took some editorial liberties in his description, the idea stuck! Your brand is the organizing principle or operating system around which all else functions. When you agree to stay true to the strategy you're working to achieve, the system works seamlessly. Deviating from the plan or being tempted away from your original goals puts the entire structure of your reputation at risk.

Additionally, think of your brand operating structure as a fluid and flexible system. While a computer's operating system may be hardwired, it must still be ready to handle updates, new peripherals and additional systems applied to it. Similarly, your brand must adapt to new situations, circumstances and opportunities. When you have a commitment to your values and brand in place, you'll be able to assess and decide on the unexpected challenges and opportunities in the context of how the parts and pieces work together, and not in a vacuum: You'll be able to clearly use this operating system to determine whether what you're evaluating is good for you or harmful, will it provide abundance or are you choosing out of fear (or scarcity), is this a healthy option to consider or are you seduced by the money involved?

*How an agreement keeps you focused*

Moving through the steps of building, pivoting or repairing your personal brand may feel like effort, or it may seem easy. It's not unheard of for someone to tell me, "Once I did the hard work of discovering, designing and putting strategy to my brand, the implementation part was easy." You'll see clearly how, where, why and when certain opportunities are right for you (and which ones aren't). The clarity you'll feel about how to present yourself, speak about your value and lead others will be notable. What seemed abstract in the past comes into focus as part of your strategy to achieve your desired brand, or not. Your personal brand agreement is where you pull reinforcements and reassurance if you need them to ensure you stay the course.

To build a personal brand agreement, consider these steps:

### 1 WRITE DOWN YOUR GOALS

While you might be tempted to type your goals into the computer on a spreadsheet, I advocate writing them down by hand. It is widely believed that transferring thoughts from your head to your hand to paper actually brings a different experience than pounding them on a keyboard. Write down on paper your desired reputation goals. Describe them in detail, painting a very clear picture with your words of what you're pursuing. You might articulate these goals in a journal, notepad, or even set of index cards—whatever form fits your needs best. The point is to write unabridged: goals, dreams, hopes, ideas and intentions of what you're striving for. Use colored pens or pencils, write in shorthand or long form, add calligraphy if you want! Just get your goals down in as much detail as you can.

If you're even more of a visual person, craft a vision board to showcase images of the goals and intentions you'll set for your life and career. A vision board can take many forms—most commonly, you take a large piece of sturdy paper or cardboard and apply to it images and words cut from magazines and other media sources. You create a collage of what you're wanting more of in your life, what you dream about and where you're headed. Many of my clients love this exercise, because it feels like when we were children and we played with glue and scissors! Place your vision board where you'll see it often. As you look at the vision board, it visually reinforces your intentions and, many argue, manifests these good things into your life.

### 2 LIST THE MANY BENEFITS YOU'LL RECEIVE AS YOU REINFORCE THIS COMMITMENT

Again, get as specific and granular as you can. What benefits, rewards or perks will you receive if you stay firm on your brand strategy? What will come from living an authentic life focused on your ideal legacy? What rewards will you attract and enjoy? Make this list specific.

Here's an example of how this might look: If your brand goal is to be known as someone who leads others with a servant's heart, a benefit you might receive is that you will hear from people you've helped with stories of how your coaching or message inspired them to do something they initially perceived as impossible. This would make you feel happy, inspired and grateful for the opportunity to make a difference for them. Resist the temptation to say, "But it's not about me. It's about them…" Yes, it will be about them, but you will receive benefits as well, as you should. Listing the benefits you'll receive will help you stay focused on the goal and will reinforce your strategy as you redeem those benefits along the way.

### 3 IDENTIFY POTENTIAL ROADBLOCKS OR OBSTACLES

As you work on your brand and desired reputation, can you already identify temptations, blind spots or weaknesses you'll need to be prepared to navigate? Are there challenges you can foresee with how you'll live your brand that you can begin to mitigate now? Most likely, the obstacles you'll have the most trouble with are the ones you can't anticipate, or the ones you're underestimating.

For example, one of my clients worked hard to clarify his personal brand goals and legacy. He was crystal clear on the values he was operating from and where he wouldn't deviate from his vision of his career. We even anticipated challenges he might encounter, and he was confident he'd be able to withstand the pressure to change his direction. Yet, when his wife became pregnant with their fourth child, and he suddenly lost his job, forcing the family to face financial uncertainty, he began entertaining job offers that were very different from his vision. He was considering working for companies that had negative reputations, where their business practices had been publicly scrutinized and criticized. While during our work together he proclaimed he could never work for a company like that, now he was seriously considering it. Luckily, his personal brand agreement helped him see what it could look like to veer away from his values and goals and realign with what he was working towards. He was able to refocus on the benefits and goals he was working towards. Eventually, he chose to take a job that paid less but aligned with his goals, which empowered him to continue to provide for his family and ride out the troublesome market his industry was facing. When the markets regained, his brand was intact and he was able to move to a better position, also in alignment with his values and goals. He hadn't compromised who he was or what he stood for, even in the face of significant personal challenge.

Plot and plan for any obstacle you can imagine challenging your reputation. Let your imagination picture the worst-case scenario. How can you envision you'd handle it? Could you stay strong in your convictions? What would you do to remind yourself of the commitment to yourself you've made today?

### 4 ENLIST A SUPPORT TEAM

To bring your brand goals into alignment and fortify your agreement, you may need help. A spouse, friend or colleague could be an excellent sounding board and reinforcement if you feel you're losing focus. Inform them of your goals, vision and the direction you're headed in, then empower them to hold you accountable, push back if they sense you're veering off course, and thank them when they do. My husband has been a great support to me as I've built my company and my brand. Many times, as I've thrashed ideas around or evaluated options, he'll remind me (in his own words) of where I came from and where I'm headed. "Is that decision or option on brand for you?"

he'll ask me, reminding me to stay true to what I know in my head and heart is the right path. Find someone (or a few people) who will do this for you. Even though your commitment is a personal one, it helps to have supporters who can be part of your process and trusted to help guide you, if needed.

### 5 CUT YOURSELF SLACK

As you build and live your personal brand and focus on your commitment to yourself and your legacy, show yourself tolerance if you deviate. It happens. Perhaps you post something online you later regret, or you hire someone who doesn't represent your values, or take a job that ends up being a blunder. Mistakes happen. Remind yourself that personal branding is not about perfection—it's about consistency. If your mistake is public, and your credibility could be questioned, refer to Chapter 6 and see what proactive steps you need to take to control the narrative, or if you can manage it more privately. You will make mistakes—everyone does. How you handle them is where your personal brand agreement will align you back with your goals. Refer to it, reflect on what led you to the error, regroup and move forward.

### 6 CELEBRATE THE MILESTONES, NO MATTER HOW SMALL

Part of your agreement to yourself must be that you'll acknowledge and celebrate the times you stay true to your brand. Reinforce those positive steps (and times you've resisted temptation) to drive them home with you. If you develop a logo that feels like you, or you are afforded a career opportunity where they refer to you by brand keywords, or you're endorsed on LinkedIn for specific qualities you want to be known by, these are markers and milestones that indicate your brand is working! Note them, celebrate them, and reward yourself for staying true to your values, brand and ultimate legacy strategy.

### An exercise to clarify your agreement

There's a helpful exercise I often use with clients to aid them in anchoring into the vision they're setting for their future. It involves first going backwards. When you're in a quiet place, free from distractions, get into a comfortable position (sitting or lying down is fine) and slow your breathing down. Take deep breaths through your nose and all the way down to your belly button, expanding your diaphragm fully. Hold the breath for a count of four, then exhale through your mouth. Do this a few times, closing your eyes if you feel comfortable.

When you are relaxed, reflect on a younger version of yourself. Whatever age you pick is fine. Go with the first one that comes to mind. Perhaps it's when you were 10 or 18 or 35. Remember who you were then and think about what you wanted, who you wanted to be when you grew up, and the hopes and dreams that motivated you. Next, have that younger version of yourself "meet" you today. Look straight into their eyes. What would they say to you? How would they feel about who you have become today? Would they be proud of who you became? What advice or guidance could they offer you?

Then, let the adult you reassure your younger self that you're okay and doing fine. You've had challenges and thrills, ups and downs, loves and losses. Through it all, you've survived and thrived. Remind them that life is a journey and you're committed to be the best version of you. Share with them the brand voyage you've been on and how important your life will be in its entirety. Assure them that you'll ensure the legacy you're both pursuing will happen, because you are fully committed to making it so. Then, watch as they smile knowing that the future is bright and you're taking every measure to live the fullest, most meaningful life for yourself, for them, and for others. You are now in control of your legacy.

How did that feel? Did it feel uplifting and empowering, or corny and silly? Either answer is fine, because the exercise is a way to ground your commitment to living your life authentically and in control. Connecting with who you were, acknowledging how far you've come, and clarifying where you're headed is a powerful way to reinforce that your brand is controllable. You have the ability and tools to influence, inspire and impact others, and drive the perception of you that highlights your value.

*Sample template agreement*

Below is a sample template agreement to consider as you craft your personal brand. In crafting your agreement, the goal is that the end product is personal and meaningful to you and will keep you committed to living your life and brand in alignment with your goals:

*My brand goal:*

*Why I'm passionate about that goal:*

*Who I'll serve:*

*Why they matter to me:*

*Where it could get challenging for me:*

*How I'll remind myself to stay focused on my goals:*

*Why success in this effort is meaningful to me:*

*Sample agreements*

As you write down your agreement, it might look something like this sample:

> *In my quest to serve the educational needs of children in my community, and be seen as a visionary leader whose expertise and experience perfectly qualify me to lead critical programs, I will remain steadfast in my passion and commitment to excellence, high achievement and compassion, ensuring that every child in our area has access to the tools and resources they need to succeed. I will likely feel pressure from stakeholders who may question my methods, or funders who'll encourage me to take shortcuts, but I'll remind myself of the faces of the children I serve and that their futures are in my hands. If I meet my goals, I will not only leave a legacy of helping those underserved populations I care about, but a child may grow up to be a leader themselves, following my example.*

Or:

*To build the personal brand I aspire to, and create my desired legacy, I will commit to:*

- *hold myself accountable to building a meaningful and impactful reputation;*
- *live authentically in all that I do—personally and professionally; move towards situations that challenge my skills and keep me learning and growing in positive, professionally healthy ways;*
- *seek out people who unapologetically pursue their dreams;*
- *being rewarded when I see evidence of the joy and love I add to the world; and*
- *take care of myself so I can care for, and lead, others as I was designed to do.*

Or:

*To be credible for my legacy of advocating for emerging leaders in our industry, whom I'm able to help see their potential and achieve their dreams, I will remain true to my core values of love, generosity and service. I will find the good in all challenges and exploit the great in all possibilities. I will force myself to confidently enter conversations that push me out of my comfort zone, I will lead by example and I will never forget that I am here to serve a purpose greater than serving myself. When I do this, I will see evidence of my contribution and feel the satisfaction in knowing I directly helped make someone else's dreams come true.*

Or:

*I am capable of building a legacy as a thoughtful and caring person, who uses innovation and technology to expand thinking and ideas. As I see that my ideas are put into motion, as I'm recognized for my contribution to science, I will remember that I deserve this legacy because I've worked hard! I can commit to living a life with integrity because it is who I am and who I was created to be.*

## Putting your agreement into action

*Evaluating opportunities through this filter*

As you evaluate opportunities and test them against your agreement, it will inevitably happen that you'll find yourself tempted to deviate from your strategy and agreement to make choices that don't support your brand positioning and legacy. Before deciding that an opportunity conflicts with your values and brand goals, check in with yourself about your thought process. Ask yourself: Is there something about this opportunity that could actually be good for me but I'm initially seeing it as a deviation from my plan? Can this actually be an indication my brand is working, but I'm being stretched to grow in new and different ways which are not actually deviation or conflict?

I had this experience many years ago. One of my biggest clients was the CEO of a large investment portfolio. I'd been asked to work with the leaders of many of the companies within his portfolio, helping them build up and promote their personal brands (sometimes including the company brand as well). One of his companies made a move that caused me to question whether my values were in alignment: The leadership of this company hired a well-known and highly outspoken woman to lead a sector of the company. She was known for her extreme political views which, to say they conflicted with my own and my values, would be an understatement. She'd been in the media spotlight often for her outlandish opinions, she seemed to relish in her radical approach, and was someone I was comfortable never meeting in person. Yet, now I was being asked to on behalf of one of my largest clients.

My client asked that I fly to the East Coast and meet with this woman to onboard her into the brand of the company and offer guidance on how she could leverage her existing high-profile reputation to adding value for the company. I couldn't believe what I was being asked to do. For days I deliberated on how to proceed. "Do I risk offending and upsetting my biggest client by refusing to work with someone I find so offputting and who's in conflict with what

I believe?" The question haunted me. I worried that if I agreed to go, I was doing it only for the money and therefore compromising my values and brand. Then I considered something profound: I could actually take baby steps towards this challenge, as I had many opportunities to leave if I needed to. Perhaps I could even learn something here that would be significant to my work. Maybe it wouldn't be as bad as I believed. Instead of seeing this as a test of my commitment to my agreement with myself, could this offer me an opportunity to stretch outside my comfort zone and grow? I knew I could help this woman, so I took a step forward.

I remember we met on a foggy October morning in Boston. I was hesitant, but open-minded. The four-hour conversation that ensued was remarkable. Yes, she was exactly the person I'd anticipated, full of highly charged opinions, ideas and theories, but she was also extremely approachable and tolerant of my reluctance. In fact, the first thing she said to me was, "I assume you've researched me and know what I'm about. Before we get to work, feel free to ask me anything about anything you've read. I'm an open book." And she was. I learned that I could work with people vastly different from myself. That I could lean into uncomfortable situations and, with my brand goals always front and center, I could proceed cautiously and with an open mind, learning much about other people.

As a brand strategist, my job isn't to be judge and jury to the clients I serve. I'm not their mother, priest or therapist. My role is to evaluate their situation, help them clarify their goals, and afford them tools and coaching to proceed. Of course, I have the right to turn down a potential client if I feel it's in my best interest or is not a good fit, and I have done so many times. I've also learned that to move towards the uncomfortable is sometimes the way to grow and elevate my skills and knowledge. I encourage you to consider the same— before you completely reject an opportunity because it scares you or feels unpleasant or makes you question why you'd proceed, consider whether it is exactly what you need, right now, to get to where you're going.

*Course-correcting if temptation leads you away from your agreement*

In the years since my brand was first tested, where I turned down the lucrative contract because I didn't see alignment with my values and brand, I've been tested other times and even a few times failed to maintain my agreement with myself. Whether agreeing to work with a client I knew wasn't compatible with my style (but I swore I could fix that!) or taking a speaking engagement for a fee lower than my standard rate (because I didn't stay firm on my value) or feeling so intimidated and impressed by a colleague that I signed a joint venture which only benefitted them, not me, I've learned from each mistake. With each step backwards, I forced myself to propel forward and to make greater strides to build up and stay in agreement with the brand I was building. In a way, the setbacks actually reinforced my brand unknowingly. Without seeing how I could learn from a misstep, it would have just been a failure. Learning from the mistake and celebrating the milestone of my confidence boost after recommitting to my brand and myself afterwards reinforces my worth and value to those individuals I'm fortunate enough to serve.

If you need to course-correct because you made a decision that is in conflict with your personal agreement, consider these steps:

1 **Recognize and acknowledge the misstep as early as possible.** Doing so will help you mitigate any damage or additional risk. Working with an investor whose ethics are questionable? Pay the penalty and end the contract. Leading a company where you are not empowered and therefore ineffective and your reputation could suffer? Consider taking the quick negative reputation hit from a bad choice and quit to find something more meaningful. Take on a client who drains your soul of all that is good? Yes, you can fire clients if need be. Put a post on social media that you later realize was inappropriate or offensive? Walk it back as quickly as possible. Delete the post, apologize to your online connections, reach out directly to anyone who told you they were upset and recommit to being more mindful about what you post.

2 **Reflect on what led you off your agreed-upon path.** Were you tempted by the money involved? Was there something about the

opportunity or situation that lured you away from what you knew was right for you? For example, were you lured off course by an opportunity to travel to exotic places but later realized that you were spending too much time away from family? In this case, your desire to travel and see more of the world could be a passion to act on but without sacrificing time with your loved ones. Be honest with yourself as you reflect on where you were tempted and lured away from the priorities you set out to meet.

3 **Reframe and recommit.** With an understanding of where you strayed from your agreement, take accountability for the behavior and recommit to your goals. Perhaps you need to update or revise your personal brand agreement. Was the first one sufficient to keep you grounded in your goals for the legacy you're pursuing? It could be that you need to include more people in your process to help hold you accountable. Do you feel your support network is attentive to your goals and encouraging you to have regular conversations about your commitment to achieve them? When you've strayed from the commitment you made to yourself, remember that the goal is to ensure you live a life (and enjoy a legacy) that is consistent with your values. You serve no one by deviating from that plan.

## In closing

There's a well-known theory called the Butterfly Effect, which proposes that the flaps of a butterfly's wings in one country could create a significant weather event in a country far away. The idea promotes the interconnectedness of actions (even minute happenings, such as the flap of the wings of a small insect) in one place with the effects and impact far away. If you ascribe to the notion that what you're doing today could impact someone far away, or that the intentions you're making now will bring bearing on others, maybe even without your knowing, you understand the idea behind the Butterfly Effect and the brand agreement. By making the agreement with yourself, you are setting the goal—the motion—of how you'll live your life and brand to achieve your desired legacy and success.

Your brand agreement is a personal commitment you make to yourself to stay the course. In creating such an agreement, you can confidently and reliably make decisions that are in alignment with your goals and values and repel those that don't. You'll be careful not to assume too quickly that something is unhealthy or "off brand" because there could be valuable learning or growing included in the opportunity which you might dismiss. You will evaluate and consider opportunities and challenges, refer to your brand agreement and proceed with confidence. Yes, you may make mistakes. But realizing the error quickly, rectifying the situation adequately and learning from the mistake is how you'll grow and continue to work towards your desired personal brand and legacy. Now, let's examine how you'll measure and monitor your personal brand to ensure you're seeing the results and impact your strategy, tactics and agreement are designed to produce.

# 08

# Measuring and monitoring reputational assets

*How do you know if your brand is producing the results you want? This chapter lays out various benchmarks and milestones to assess brand effectiveness and offers suggestions for modifying brand strategy when results are inadequate.*

## Understanding reputation metrics

Is it possible or reasonable to expect we can measure and quantify something as intangible as reputation? "Is it like measuring love?" I was once asked. Interestingly, it is a bit. Just as love is a powerful feeling that is either there or it isn't, has different degrees of intensity, and varies from a mother's love for a child to a soldier's love of country to my own love of chocolate, reputation is also variable and highly powerful in its emotional qualities. Measuring reputation is as much art as it is science. As we've discussed earlier in this book, why someone feels the way they do, or perceives you a certain way, has a lot to do with their emotional filters, biases, capacity for those feelings and the influences of previous experiences. There are reputation indicators, however, which help us gauge how easily found we are by our target audience, ways external perception influences our effectiveness and impact with others, and whether our target communities will engage with our brand or find us irrelevant. We find many of these tools online, but some remain in things like referrals, testimonials, client satisfaction and endorsements made by people who interact with us in person.

In traditional public relations work, the measurement of brand reach and reputation is often quantified in number of views, share of voice and quality of the engagement. These metrics represent the number of times your brand is talked about divided by the industry or category you seek to impact and include analysis of the quality of the audience and whether or not the interaction was positive (a glowing recommendation for you on your LinkedIn profile, for instance) or negative (hateful post about your services, for example, on a review site). This number typically looks at online followers, connections and "friends" and evaluates their relevancy by the quality of the profile. For example, a profile that is not in a qualified category (i.e., target audience) might receive a lower score than a profile of an ideal new client for you.

Today, with social media, measuring reputation online is challenged because, to measure quality, we must know something about the person posting the information or comment, and people online are not always truthful or revealing about their intentions. As we discussed in Chapter 6, a negative review about your work on your company's website or a review website may have come from a disgruntled employee, online hacker, petty competitor or it may have actually come from an unhappy client. Sometimes it's almost impossible to detect. The steps you take to remedy those situations will certainly depend on the circumstances and options at your disposal, depending on the platform.

## Creating the metrics

*Outlining and measuring tactics to meet your goals*

Your strategy should contain the detailed steps you'll focus on to bring your personal brand to life and build your desired reputation. Then, you can measure and track effectiveness of each step, evaluate how well the steps and tools work together, and course-correct if needed. Following is a sample set of tactics you might create, along with sample metrics, to build your brand and evaluate effectiveness.

## NARRATIVE

### Spoken

- Do you feel you are in control of your spoken narrative?
- Do you have a clear elevator pitch?
- Has your elevator pitch been modularized to be relatable and meet the needs of different audiences?
- Have you received positive feedback on your elevator pitch? What do you qualify as a positive outcome from your pitch?
- Can you deliver your elevator pitch clearly and with confidence?
- Have you practiced your elevator pitch with others, and received feedback on its effectiveness and impact?

Rate the overall effectiveness of your spoken narrative (1 lowest; 5 highest).

### Written

- Are your professional biography, CV and résumé written to be in alignment with your personal brand goals?
- Do you have a targeted speaker introduction ready to go if you are called to present in public?
- If you write publications, is your biography for each one consistent with your brand goals?
- Are your emails reflecting the tone and posturing of your brand?
- Do you have a consistent and memorable email signature, consistent with your brand?

Rate the overall effectiveness of your written narrative (1 lowest; 5 highest).

Online

- Are your online profiles written to be consistent with your personal brand goals and positioning? Is the tone consistent across platforms?
- Is your website or blog written in the same nature, imagery and positioning as your other content online?
- Are you showing up in a Google search for the "news" you want?
- Are there any negative results from a Google search on your name?
- Is someone with the same name showing up in a Google search for you?
- Have you set up a Google Alert for yourself with versions of the spelling of your name, if needed?

Rate the overall effectiveness of your online narrative (1 lowest; 5 highest).

### ONLINE POSITIONING AND DIGITAL CAPITAL

- For each platform you're active on, how many followers and connections do you currently have? (If your targeted platform offers connections and followers, as LinkedIn does, list both.)
- Are most of your connections qualified buyers or networking contacts?
- How would you rate the effectiveness of your online engagement? How regularly do people interact with, respond to and share your content?
- Do you seek to measure "likes" instead of engagement? Be specific about how you'll evaluate engagement.
- How frequently are you posting, sharing and updating your online content?
- Are you writing and posting articles and blogs?
- Are you sharing content by others, with introductory narrative that shares your view or position on the content?
- Are you fully vetting any information or content you share from others (to ensure you are entirely aware of what's contained in the post)?

- Do you regularly comment on other people's posts? Are you getting engagement on your comments?
- Do you regularly and publicly celebrate and acknowledge the success of others (and share their posts) online?
- Are others talking about you and your brand more today than previously? Are those comments positive or negative?
- Are online audiences referring to you online by your keywords and key phrases?
- Have you received viable business offers or ideas through your online network? How do you define the "value" of that offer?

Rate the overall effectiveness of your online positioning and digital capital (1 lowest; 5 highest).

STRATEGIC NETWORKING

Targeted events

- Are you attending in-person events to advance your positioning and help you meet key target contacts?
- Are you regularly researching in advance the events you attend to ensure you meet the right people?
- Do you have a follow-up strategy in place before you go to an event?

Rate the effectiveness of your participation in targeted networking events (1 lowest; 5 highest).

Current contacts

- Do you believe you know the right people?
- Do you have an active list of your contacts in a searchable format (i.e., Excel spreadsheet or customer relationship management (CRM) tool)?
- How many people do you know right now who can and would help advance you in your career and brand goals? Are they tagged as such in your database?

- Who do you need to know?
- Do you have a game plan for how you will meet them?
- How will you determine, then explore, synergies with new prospects?
- Do you have an enticing offer or pitch to draw in new contacts?

Rate the effectiveness of your relationships with current contacts (1 lowest; 5 highest).

## Curating new relationships

- How many in-person meetings are you having each week with new contacts?
- How many phone calls are you having each month with prospects?
- Are you sending notes, cards, gifts and acknowledgments of key milestones in your networking contacts' lives?
- Have you communicated where you are and where you're headed to this network?
- How confident are you that if an ideal opportunity for you presented itself to your network, they would think of you and refer you?
- Does your network refer, endorse and provide testimony to your brand goals?

Rate the effectiveness of your strategies to curate new relationships (1 lowest; 5 highest).

### PRESENCE

- Does your current "look" represent who you are today?
- Do you have a signature style? Have you ensured it is updated?
- If your role or career has changed, have you modified your look and wardrobe to be appropriate to where you are now?
- If your body or style has changed, have you updated your wardrobe?

- If your reputation has been challenged because of your appearance and presence, have you taken steps to correct the issues?
- Have you identified certain outfits that make you feel powerful and confident? Are those outfits clean and ready to put on at any time?
- Is your body language consistent with your desired positioning?
- If you've received feedback on negative body language issues or challenges with your gestures or movements, have you addressed those?

Rate the effectiveness of presence in supporting your brand goals (1 lowest; 5 highest).

Next, list all of your ratings to see how you're doing:

- Effectiveness of your spoken narrative: 1–2–3–4–5
- Effectiveness of your written narrative: 1–2–3–4–5
- Effectiveness of your online narrative: 1–2–3–4–5
- Effectiveness of your online positioning and digital capital: 1–2–3–4–5
- Effectiveness of your strategic networking at targeted events: 1–2–3–4–5
- Effectiveness of your relationships with current contacts: 1–2–3–4–5
- Effectiveness of your strategies to curate new relationships: 1–2–3–4–5
- Effectiveness of your presence: 1–2–3–4–5

If your answers range from 8–12, you'd be advised to revisit your goals and clarify the action steps more carefully. This score could indicate you've either not articulated in enough detail how to achieve the goals, are wavering in your commitment to the plan, or need to assign more focus and effort to driving these results.

A score of 30–40 is a good indicator that you're on the right track and should maintain focus on what's been working. Where are you scoring the highest? Where are you the weakest? Just because you are highest in one area doesn't mean you can rest on that success. This process requires constant effort and evaluation. The platforms or outlets might shift or change, your time availability might slide, so be sure to spend the most effort on what works best, without ignoring the other opportunities. A great example of how this works is what happened in 2020, when the world shut down because of the COVID-19 pandemic. If someone had previously focused all of their effort and attention on in-person networking and relationship-building to drive their career, visibility and brand, now they would be hard-pressed to leave the house. As everyone sheltered in place around the world, that person would have been well advised to build up their online presence or risk losing out. As previously mentioned, the tactics in your personal brand strategy are not isolated tools—they work well when integrated with the others to paint a holistic picture of who you are, what you value and where you can add impact.

## Ongoing feedback: additional assessments

In previous chapters, we've reviewed the importance of soliciting feedback on your brand from people you trust and assessing the perception they have of your value. The feedback exercise is a power-ful way to weigh how you're perceived and the distance between where you are and where you'd like to be. Now, as you look to meas-ure the impact and efficacy of your brand strategy, feedback also plays a role in your ongoing development. Ongoing feedback may repeat the process you did before, by deploying survey tools in email or online, or you could even consider repeating the same questions to gauge your efficacy on moving perception if you desired.

### REPEAT FEEDBACK SURVEYS

To repeat the surveys, reassure your original recipients that their initial insights were valuable and impactful in helping you create a strategy to live authentically and intentionally. Remind them that they participated before and now you're asking for an updated set of feedback responses to determine if you've shifted in areas you felt needed help and strengthened areas where you were already growing strong. As always, thank them for considering the request and hopefully they will once again offer you valuable insight. Their new feedback surveys will reveal if their perception of you changed for the better, stayed the same or deteriorated. Either way, the data is helpful to you as you evaluate your progress.

## 360 EVALUATIONS

As part of your work, you might receive surveys such as 360 evaluations. These tools are designed to provide recipients with a holistic view of how they are perceived by coworkers, staff, managers and other stakeholders at work, with additional feedback included. The questions solicit input on a variety of areas of professional development, skills, performance, leadership potential and growth projection. If deployed and debriefed correctly, a 360 evaluation can offer the recipient a comprehensive look at their career impact and identify areas for growth and improvement. This tool is traditionally implemented by a professional trained in administering the survey and debriefing on the feedback.

In my opinion, there are advantages and disadvantages to the 360 evaluation. If done correctly, the instrument can help the recipient identify blind spots and opportunities for improvement and growth, can initiate a dialog between coworkers and foster collaboration, mentoring and learning, can reinforce or promote self-development (self-awareness often starts the process of self-development among career-oriented professionals) and elevate accountability as strengths and weaknesses are now publicly noted. On the negative side, when a 360 evaluation is not deployed or debriefed correctly, the recipient can experience damaged self-esteem, may question their work relationships, feel singled out and could possibly quit a good situation. Also, if the work culture is toxic or hostile, feedback can be skewed; if relationships aren't healthy, results will be misleading; and if it focuses too heavily on negative input, the individual might not see how to resolve the challenges and might internalize the negativity as criticism.

INFORMAL FEEDBACK

Here, we're speaking of feedback that might be more anecdotal and informal. Gossip, word of mouth, "word on the street" and even rumors can count as informal feedback. What are people saying about you when you're not there? How do they regard you and your contribution? Are you hearing from others that your team, board of directors, investors or other target audiences are perceiving you differently today than before? Is that difference aligned with your goals or in the opposite direction of them? When you approach a group and are received by them, is their reception more or less positive than it was previously? This type of informal feedback should influence your assessment of progress (or retreat) but not be the sole basis—if you sense the informal feedback shows you're not making progress, then a more formal assessment may be warranted to confirm, or dispel, your suspicions.

## Assessing progress towards desired reputation

*Evaluating your progress*

When assessing your progress towards your desired brand, the goal is to identify milestones to show forward movement. If you receive confirmation that, yes, you are starting to earn the legacy you strive for, that's a win! When you get hints that you may not be making progress, or might be headed in the wrong direction, you'll note this and course-correct. Here's an example of how this might work: In working with my client, Tina, we decided that to build her brand as a caring, compassionate and talented psychotherapist, focused on providing a safe space and holistic approach to treating issues facing at-risk youth, we would focus on social media to engage her target audiences. She had three specific audiences we'd approach: One audience she sought to attract were youth who might be struggling. She also targeted the parents of young people who might not identify that their child was in danger. Another group included teachers and professionals who might interact with young people who were struggling. Tina's approach for the young people was to show how, when, where and why they should seek help if they felt they needed it. Keywords we used in her social media strategy for her brand included: safety, risk, troubled, youth, addiction and recovery (many of these youth had been through recovery programs).

For the parents, the strategy was less critical and more supportive (she wanted parents to look for signs their teen was at risk and feared that if they felt judged as "bad parents" they might miss important warning signs). For teachers and other professionals, Tina wanted them to see that she's a resource, a partner to them, and not a threat who would strip them of their authority. Most importantly, for the young people (mostly aged 12–19), her message was, "Life is rough. You're not alone. I am a safe place. I can help," and messages to that effect. We targeted young people on sites like Facebook, Snapchat and Instagram. The parents were targeted on Facebook and a bit on LinkedIn. The teachers and other professionals were found on LinkedIn, Twitter, Facebook and Instagram. Posts were a blend of images, graphics, video and straight-text posts offering statistics around youth suicide and addiction, hope for someone struggling, families reunited after a crisis, etc. Overall, the messages were caring, compassionate and full of hope. For each platform and each target audience, we measured several metrics:

- Number of inbound inquiries to Tina's office (phone or web)— each call, web form or email was queried: How did you find us? And if it came through social media channels, we noted which one.

- Number of "likes"—this gave us some indication of the community's approval of the content of a post.

- Number of comments—then, we'd look at the quality of the comments: Were they engaging with the content, or simply saying "cool" or "great info"? We evaluated the quality of the engagement further.

- Number of shares—this, for Tina, was most meaningful. Was a parent sharing the message with a child? Was a friend sharing the post with a friend they worried about? Was a teacher sharing the post with a community?

For each target audience, for each platform and for each post, the numbers of each category were measured, but we dug deep into quality. Were people who liked the posts more apt to call Tina's office? Did more people who shared the information end up following her pages rather than lurking anonymously? And, did the people who sought support and treatment originate from a specific message or campaign, were they long-time connections, or did they just find her and take action? Each of these metrics provided insight and value to her brand positioning.

### What else can you measure?

Anecdotally, you can measure how you're introduced to others. I remember walking into a business networking meeting and someone greeted me with "Lida, the generosity queen," and I knew they were picking up on a specific keyword I was focused on (generosity). Had they introduced me as "Lida, the marketing pro," I might have been happy they got my industry correct, but the keyword would have been off.

You'll also measure the referrals and references you receive. When someone sends me a client referral, for instance, one of the first questions I ask is, "What did they tell you about me and my work?" My goal is to understand how clearly my referring sources understand my work product, but also my goals, passion and unique value. Similarly, on LinkedIn, you can receive written recommendations from people who wish to endorse you. When a recommendation comes in, check it for keywords and key phrases that are aligned with your brand strategy and desired legacy. If the recommendation doesn't include any of those key phrases or words, or deviates from the focus you're promoting, it is perfectly acceptable to ask the sender to revise their endorsement. This happened for Wyatt, who received a recommendation from one of his financial clients on his LinkedIn profile. The client noted his great sense of humor and the ability to reach him day or night with a question or concern. While both of these qualities were true, Wyatt didn't want to be seen as taking work lightly or setting the expectation that all clients could call him at all hours. He asked that the client revise the recommendation (if they felt comfortable) to focus on his desired keywords: knowledgeable (about financial planning), passionate (about financial literacy and empowering his clients) and client-focused in his approach. The client was happy to revise their written recommendation and Wyatt's reputation grew.

You may also seek to measure and monitor the quality of the prospects you're attracting. If your goal is to attract a more sophisticated client, who will place high value on your expertise, knowledge and commitment to their success, you may be monitoring your ability to attract those clients by how you're positioning yourself online and in person. Are you being seen in the right circles, at the right events, rubbing shoulders with the right people? Are you interviewing clients who you know aren't right for you, but you're motivated by the possibility they can pay your fees? Are you creating too much of a retail brand approach online (this might mean you're putting coupons, sales and special offers on your services)?

## Modifying your metrics when needed

You've likely detected that the idea of course-correcting is a common thread in building, pivoting and repairing reputation. If you approach the strategy of building your brand and reputation as a rigid and inflexible process, you could make costly mistakes. When you view the process as fluid and adaptable, you'll see the advantages of course-correcting as a solution to unforeseen challenges or obstacles. Your strategy might morph, the marketplace could deteriorate or expand, your life circumstances may look different, requiring your approach to be modified. You could find it impossible or unrealistic to deploy the strategy you've committed to or your ability to fulfill your legacy is challenged because of a traumatic event. Sometimes course-correcting is warranted. The most notable times to need to change direction are when something goes really wrong with your brand approach (i.e., you may have missed something in your assessment phase, making it unrealistic to build towards your desired brand) or when your goals or needs change significantly (i.e., perhaps your market shifts, making your value proposition obsolete).

When modifying your original goals or strategy, be sure to adjust your metrics for success. If you create more ambitious goals, add milestones to watch for and revise the ones you initially created. Perhaps the metrics you set out at the beginning are too easy to achieve and you need to "raise the bar" higher now. Remind yourself that even if you fall short of your larger goals, you'll likely experience more growth, opportunity and brand recognition than if you set your sights on smaller, more attainable goals. It's okay to stretch, to be ambitious and to want to "change the world." The worst that can happen if you don't get there completely is that you've positively impacted and helped a lot of people along the way.

If course-correcting or adjusting your strategy is imminent, find allies to lean on during the process. The support systems you've built for yourself, personally and professionally, are vested in seeing you happy and successful. When you need to make a change—a small one or a significant shift—in how you'll build your brand and measure results, enlist their insight and help. It's likely someone in your support system has faced a similar challenge or twist in their plan. Ask them about their process, the steps they took, what they did right and what they wish they hadn't done. Lean on them for advice, guidance and mentoring, but retain all decision-making. After all, you did the hard work to create the strategy and you are responsible for living your brand to the fullest.

## In closing

Hopefully this chapter provided you with many ideas, tools, checklists and resources to evaluate the efficacy and impact of your personal brand as you build it. Nothing, however, can provide you with a better sense of how you're doing, where you're headed and how you're showing up than looking inward. Most people aren't great at seeing their own weaknesses and flaws, but when challenged with which way to go, which option to choose, what feels right and what feels off, remember to trust your internal moral and brand compass, and refer to your agreement, which will not let you down. Refer to your measurements of success—from social media "likes" to referrals to endorsements to career opportunities that seem to appear out of thin air—and remind yourself to stay the course.

Measuring and monitoring the results of your brand strategy will give you the confidence you'll need to remain on track with your plan. As you see the number and quality of your followers rise, the consistent reference to your narrative, the growth of your online engagement, the positive impression your presence and body language create, and the value to your career of your narrative and network, you'll be assured you're making progress. When something feels off course or needs adjusting, you'll be able to pinpoint where that shift needs to happen and won't risk changing what is working to fix what isn't.

# 09

# Reputation risk management

*Once you've built your brand, how do you maintain it, identify risk and nurture opportunity? Here, you will learn how to manage ongoing reputation tactics and ensure any risks are diminished.*

I remember the moment like it was yesterday: I was angry about something that had happened at work with a colleague, and on a walk around the neighborhood to blow off steam I'd mentally crafted the perfect post to share on Facebook and LinkedIn to share my frustration. Carefully crafted and cryptic enough to get the attention of the person my anger was directed at, I was confident others wouldn't see my post as rage, but rather as sarcasm and even wit. I sat down at the computer, opened the Facebook app, and paused. I knew better than to send a message online that could, in fact, get me in trouble. Even if it was a long shot anyone else would see through my humor and get the implication of the angry message, I couldn't take the chance that I could be perceived as spiteful. My reputation is too precious. I closed the computer and reminded myself that managing reputation risk is more important than a fleeting moment of vengeful gratification.

You've now spent the time, effort and resources to build, pivot or repair your reputation, and managing and maintaining a healthy reputation is critical to ensuring your reputation is intact and sustainable. This is no time to take your eye off the prize and coast into a successful career. Reputation risk management is a constant and evolving effort that helps you avoid mistakes, upright any missteps and stay focused on building your ideal desired brand. Here, we will examine some of the steps to take to ensure the perception others have of you continues to align with your goals, even in the face of challenge.

## Understanding reputation risk management

### *What is reputation risk management?*

In business, the term "reputation risk management" is as common as "profits and losses" or "operations." Companies know that to maintain a healthy and viable relationship and experience with their customers and to continually deliver on expectations to stay competitive, they must anticipate and manage any risk that could jeopardize the brand. As much as can be foreseen, businesses prepare and plan for situations that could put the trust their customer has with them at risk. Sometimes the threats are more obvious, such as when a flight attendant yells at a customer and other passengers video tape the incident, putting the airline's "customer first" values in question. In other cases, as happened to Equifax in 2017 when a huge data breach put the financial records of 140+ million consumers at risk,[1] the scale of events that unfolded could be argued are less predictable. In either case, however, a reputation response team is quickly deployed to mitigate and try to stop credibility and customer trust from hemorrhaging.

For individuals, reputation risk management also necessitates being able to predict threats, anticipate changes or situations which could cause harm or negative impressions, and have strategies and responses ready to go in the event of a crisis or dramatic shift. For an individual who has previously endured a hostile work environment, for instance, and had to rebuild their credibility after attacks caused their values to be challenged, they may enter their next job with the memories of what unfolded, along with appropriate responses, to empower them to handle any future work conflicts that resemble what they went through. But many of us haven't had to endure a reputation risk in the past, so proactively creating one and being mindful of how to respond are important.

### Reputation risk management means good brand hygiene

Over time, identifying and managing risks to your personal brand and reputation become more habitual and familiar. With practice it becomes more instinctual and "normal" to filter and think about your actions in advance.

For example, after finishing his personal branding work, a professional athlete client I worked with noted, "I find myself pausing before doing things I used to do casually." He told me how he now reviews invitations to connect online because he wants to see who the person is, the kinds of things they post about and who they are connected to. He told me:

> In the past, I'd just accept any invitation to connect. Now, I see that I'm known by the people I associate with and I have to be careful. I don't want the wrong people creeping into my network and hurting the brand I'm working hard to build.

He also considers how he posts and shows up online. He said:

> I've started a 24-hour rule for all my posts. When I video or write something I want to share with my online networks and fans, I now wait 24 hours to think about it. Sometimes, that time makes me realize that something I thought was funny could be seen as insensitive or off-brand. In other cases, holding off the need to share something quickly has saved me from sharing information that was premature or confidential. I love this system of self-management for my brand!

The following is a list of areas to pay attention to and manage to protect your personal brand. While this list is exhaustive, it's not all-inclusive. Your personal brand strategy and goals will drive what to watch out for, how you should engage with others, and when a risk becomes a real threat to you and your brand. As you explore the following areas for reputation risk, add others you'll need to pay attention to, and eliminate ones that aren't important or relevant for you to monitor to ensure reputation risk is lessened.

## Managing reputation risk

*At work and in your career*

Undoubtedly, your professional career reputation is an area you'll be concerned with as you either elevate your career stature and reputation, change direction of your professional brand or repair your reputation. Managing risk and being in control of how you are perceived by others is an ongoing process, and is directed by how you show up, engage with others, consistently communicate your value and make choices that support your values (or are in conflict with them). Here, focus on how you are at work, in business or professional settings, and how you assess risk in your career:

1 **Watch for conflicts of interest.** Be mindful of forming relationships with peers, clients, vendors or influencers who could be perceived as having alternative motives or suggest a conflict of interest with your brand, work or values. Even the perception of a conflict can be troublesome for your current clients, staff and stakeholders in your business and reputation. If you network with competitors, for instance, make it clearly known that you value inclusivity and collaboration, so as to not create the wrong impression about your commitment to your work. If you choose to associate with clients who have tarnished reputations, help your network see that you're trying to help them or remind your network and prospective clients that "there are two sides to every story" and perhaps there's more to the negative reputation than is known. Always control the narrative about why you'd associate with people whose reputation is less than stellar, before you fall victim to guilt by association or perceived conflict of interest.

2 **Pay attention to negative press** (media) your employer, associates, investors and board receive. Similar to what can happen with a

perceived conflict of interest, you can be regarded as guilty by association when someone close to you or your employer is negatively portrayed in the media. Evaluate whether the article or news story is a headline piece that will likely grow to ongoing stories or is a small mention in an otherwise innocuous post. The veracity and popularity of the piece can direct your choice of whether you plan a response or wait it out and see what unfolds. Negative social media reviews about your company can bleed into adverse impressions of who you are and what you value (after all, you work for the company). Make it a habit to periodically check sites like Glassdoor, Facebook and Yelp for reviews your employer, associates or any volunteer organizations you're attached to might receive. In some cases, clients have had to resign from their company, or board of directors, because of negative press those entities received that wasn't directly attached to them and their work but they ran the risk of reputation risk by association.

3 **Sudden or unexpected loss of key relationships** or allies should be managed for perception. Lose a big client? Parting ways with a business partner? Resigning your job to spend more time with family? These types of event can lead to speculation and rumor about your viability, commitment and choices. Get ahead of this news by having a well-thought-out and strategic narrative to share immediately. If media or online groups run with the story, and speculate why the change, you may find yourself in a defensive, rather than offensive, posture where you are controlling how the message is shared.

4 **Ensure your skills, talents and knowledge are current and valued.** Periodically assess your own competencies, contribution and value and their relevancy to how your work and leadership are regarded. Do you need to upskill your abilities and knowledge to remain competitive in your field? Are your talents recognized and valued in your current role? Watch how others around you are positioning their knowledge and abilities and whether they are getting more attention and recognition. This could be an indication you need to step up your game to be relevant. Before you become seen as

obsolete or irrelevant, take control over your career by doing your own due diligence on what the market (and your company) needs and how your contribution and leadership are creating exponential value.

5 **Continually seek input, feedback and data on how your brand is being communicated.** It's tempting to think we are the best judge of our brand, but really it is the perception your target audience holds that matters. From time to time, seek opportunities to evaluate and assess how your brand is working and whether adjustments need to be made to your brand strategy to get you the results you seek. Pay attention to the feedback, rumors or insights of your customers, clients, team and other stakeholders. And listen to gossip, rumors or speculation from your target audience. While it might be hard to hear, there could be valuable insights in what you overhear or what is shared candidly in more relaxed environments. The point of this kind of feedback (gossip) is to learn from it. Some people aren't included in traditional feedback processes or might be resistant to share insights in formal documentation (i.e., performance evaluations and reviews) but will share their concerns and feelings in more casual settings. In Chapter 8 we looked at ways to monitor and measure brand impact. Use those tools and techniques to gain insight about your reputation and test your beliefs about how you're known by the audiences you seek to inform, influence, inspire and impact professionally.

*In your personal life*

Our personal lives undoubtedly impact our professional work and reputation. If you are distracted, unhappy or unfulfilled personally, there is a strong chance you won't show up professionally as your best self, be interested in healthy options at work, and could self-sabotage your career. Similarly, when you feel supported, encouraged and healthy at home, you'll likely bring a more positive and optimistic attitude to your choices and work. Here are some ways to manage and mitigate risk in your life outside of work:

1 **Assess your feelings of resilience and adaptability.** Do you have a support network to encourage and care for you? Are you surrounding yourself with people and situations outside of work that make you feel powerful and confident? Resilience and adaptability can grow out of circumstances or we can intentionally set out to learn how to thrive in the face of challenges and obstacles. Consider how resilient you feel, and whether you need to amplify this aspect of your life to give you more confidence and the ability to sustain challenges in all aspects of your life. To mitigate risk in your reputation, a strong foundation and base in your personal life are important.

2 **Is your personal life impacting your professional work?** If you are stressed or unhappy at home, is this causing you to be less effective at work? Sometimes, when home challenges impact your outlook on the future, preoccupy your thoughts during the work day, or impact your openness to new relationships or opportunities, it can be damaging to your brand and reputation. Life will happen, and things will get challenging from time to time. How you handle the stress is critical to reputation risk management.

    Case in point: When the pandemic shut down travel and businesses for much of 2020, I found myself grinding to a sudden halt in my work because I stressed the uncertainty in my life—personally and professionally. I'd been accustomed to traveling and speaking at conferences, corporate events and meetings around the United States. I spent time collaborating with colleagues in other industries and coaching clients in countries all over the world. My family and friends supported and encouraged me, and I loved the fast pace of my growing company. And suddenly all of that stopped. Not only did I have to manage my own stress and fears over this new situation, but my family struggled with their new realities as they adjusted to working remotely and sought guidance and support from me. I felt like I was in a circus act, spinning all the plates, making sure none fell and crashed to the ground.

During this time, I watched colleagues share their messages online of uplift and encouragement ("you can do this!") or despair and fear ("what if the world never resumes?") and wondered what my own voice should be. I opted to refrain from joining either party, really. I didn't want to focus on the doom and gloom messages by adding my feelings, which was certainly not the brand image I strived for. And, while I shared a few supportive messages, letting my online colleagues and networks know I was still available and ready to work as needed, I resisted posting incessant messages of cheery uplift and encouragement. And I increased my volunteer mentoring of military veterans significantly. I thought coaching and helping others (for free) would serve to keep me distracted and would remind me of my skills and talents. I leaned on my family for support and made sure, each and every day, that the stress and fear I was experiencing wouldn't show up in my work product. It took a lot of effort just to manage that set of emotions. I shared authentic posts about hope and support for those suffering, but my brand agreement directed me to be part of the conversation, without fueling fear, negativity or vapid encouragement.

3 **Do those around you support you?** In strategic networking, we routinely assess and cull contacts who no longer serve us. Maybe they aren't adding value to our career any longer, perhaps their choices or behavior don't align with our goals, or their treatment of us no longer brings value and purpose. Do the same with your personal life. Building and growing a strategic reputation requires you to be surrounded by people who care for you, encourage and support you. If you don't currently have those people in your life, find them. If you do have them, reward, celebrate and acknowledge them. A personal support system of people who can comfort you, cheer you on and help you think through options and challenges is crucial to a viable personal brand. Not having such people in your life can put your reputation at risk as you could begin to feel isolated in your pursuit of your ideal legacy and fail to see the impact of your legacy for those you'll leave behind when you're gone.

4 **Empower the people around you to offer you candid feedback** and input if they spot a risk or threat to your reputation. If you trust your personal support network, let them know you value their insight, judgment and opinions on your progress towards your desired brand. Inform them of your goals and strategy, and then ask them to check in with you periodically to assess your progress. Listen to their input and insights, refrain from making excuses or becoming defensive, and evaluate their suggestions or feedback against your goals and strategy.

5 **Teach your family members to be mindful and intentional about their own reputation management.** If your children are active on social media, for example, show them how to make good choices in what they post, share and comment on. This ensures you aren't at risk of being caught in the cross-hairs of something they share or promote that's inappropriate. Teach those in your close network of friends and family how to represent themselves consistent with their values and alert them if you see a misstep. This protects you from a poor choice on their part impacting your own reputation.

## Deploy your strategy and tactics to manage risk

Moving through the steps and stages of your personal brand, you will use tactics specifically designed to build, enhance and reinforce your reputation. Let's look at how you can manage reputation risk for each tactic.

### Through your narrative

Your narrative, remember, is the story you'll share with others about who you are, what you can offer and what you value. Evaluate your narrative and ability to communicate your value by reminding yourself about:

1 **The truthfulness of what you communicate.** If you find yourself consistently authentic and honest, you are at less risk for reputation

damage. If you lie, stretch the truth or find it hard to consistently be sincere, you could eventually be trapped in a mistruth, or have your dishonesty exposed, making for a reputation crisis. Transparency is not the same as truthfulness. You and your strategy are driving how transparent and forthcoming you need to be about your goals, passions and desires. But, when challenged or questioned, ensure you're being truthful about who you are and what you stand for as you communicate your narrative.

2  **Your ability to live up to the expectations you set with the target audiences** with whom you seek to earn credibility. Are you setting expectations with the people you serve that are realistic and attainable? If you give your word to someone, or say you'll represent them or endorse them, do you fulfill that promise? Your target audience might forgive one or two infractions, but over time your credibility and ability to rebuild trust could suffer if you fail to meet the expectations you set in your narrative.

3  **How people who endorse and refer you speak about your brand.** So much of the power of personal branding comes from testimonials and referrals from influencers. When someone endorses you to others and they speak the exact narrative you desire, they reinforce your positioning. Seek opportunities to correct your target audience if they speak of you differently from how you want to be known. Similarly, thank them and reinforce when they refer you using the words and positioning you desire.

4  **How confident you sound when you speak about yourself,** your brand, your accomplishments and your goals. Are you communicating power and clarity or hesitancy and weakness as you speak about your story? To control the narrative, you must be clear and confident about the story you tell others because that's the story they will share with more people as they talk about you and build your reputation.

## Relationships and network

Just like with narrative, it's critical to become intentional and focused in how your reputation could become at risk through your in-person and online relationships. Become mindful and thoughtful about the way you're showing up in networking situations, meetings and with your peers as you build your brand. Consider:

1 **The people you associate with should support your brand.** If you were a business, you'd concern yourself with supply chain and associated risk: If someone in your supply chain became compromised, it could threaten your operations. Similarly, if the people in your network, who provide you with information, contacts, support and influence, disappear or are compromised, the viability of your reputation could be at risk. Consider the reputations and actions of the people you engage with and whether they offer you credibility or threat. Carefully consider the influencers, associates, colleagues and partners you attach your name to and periodically assess their risk to your reputation.

2 **Evaluate every new contact.** Before forming a business venture, deciding to strategically network with or becoming close to a new business colleague, ask yourself how much you really know about them. Research their background and goals, and work to spot any potential conflicts or risks to you if you associate with them. Doing so can also unveil ideas and thoughts on how you might expand or grow the relationship and will help identify anything that seems too good to be true or misleading.

3 **Be mindful of the problems you help your target audience solve.** Regularly assess your target audience's needs and wants and consider how closely your value proposition aligns. Make sure you weave solutions, ideas and offers into your conversations and networking. And, check to be sure your target audience's goals haven't shifted away from the value proposition and brand you're promoting. This could jeopardize your ability to build and maintain credibility and relevancy with them.

4 **Remind yourself to listen and learn.** If you find yourself doing all the talking when meeting new contacts or visiting with colleagues and networking contacts, you're likely not learning how they can help you and what they can offer. With each engagement and opportunity, seek to learn and understand more and more. This practice will not only help you avoid roadblocks which could be approaching, but will also help you grow and expand your skills, knowledge and understanding of what's important to the audiences you want to serve.

5 **Stay mindful of how you feel around certain people.** There are likely to be those people you're with who make you feel excited, happy, confident and proud. And then there are those who might make you feel insecure, inadequate, self-conscious or sad. These feelings could be your intuition telling you the relationship is not healthy or good for you and your reputation. Always take note of those feelings, do your research, ask yourself the hard questions (e.g., why am I spending time with this person? What do I gain? What do I fear if I end the relationship?) and, if needed, move on. ·

## Online

Online conversations tend to move fast and as we work to keep up with exchanges, stay relevant, top of mind and engaged with our networks, we can make costly reputation mistakes. Instead of feeling the pressure to be the first to comment on a post or idea, or the first to share or make a post, remember these tips:

1 **Before you share, comment or engage with a post you see on social media, read the entire message,** click through the link, verify the content and read some of the other comments shared. A colleague of mine told me of an experience that almost jeopardized her job and reputation. She saw a post about helpful training resources for new parents of German shepherd puppies, her favorite breed. She knew the person who posted it was a respected dog breeder, and not only did my colleague click "like" on the post, but she shared it with her network with an enthusiastic "this is great" message.

After a few hours, someone in her network phoned her with an alarming, "Did you seriously share a link to an animal abuse video?" My colleague hadn't vetted the link, but rather assumed (since she thought she knew the sender) that it was legitimate and would be helpful to share. Her colleagues at work also noticed the post, and her employer seriously questioned her judgment and discretion. The dog breeder's account, it was revealed, had been hacked, but my colleague was responsible for endorsing and then promoting the content. Luckily, she was able to explain her way out of a reputation crisis and recover. The lesson is: Always read the entire post, check the link and consider the impact of the content to your own reputation before promoting it. Some online users will actually spread a post of mostly legitimate content, burying something offensive or inappropriate at the end of the post assuming no one will read that far before sharing it. Avoid this classic mistake.

2  **Set up a Google Alert.** By visiting Google.com/Alerts, you can enter your name and receive notifications from Google when content, images or mentions about you appear online. While not foolproof, a Google Alert can help you be one of the first to know if something about you shows up online. I also encourage clients to periodically enter their name into the search bar on an internet browser to see if additional mentions or information appears about them. Be sure to check the "news" tab as well as "images" to see what's making headlines, where your name is linked or mentioned, and what images are attributed to you and your likeness. Staying ahead of what appears online about you is crucial to being able to identify and respond to negative online information.

3  **Read the analytics.** If you maintain a blog or website, get into the habit of reviewing the analytics. Who's visiting your site? How long are they staying on critical pages? Where are they coming to your site from? This is helpful information to gauge interest in you and your work. Additionally, sites like LinkedIn offer unique dashboards of analytics on the traffic, engagement and opportunities you're seeing through their platform. Review these regularly to

adjust or refine your self-marketing as needed to drive the results you desire.

4  **Use a consistent name across social media.** I had a client once who used a formal name on LinkedIn, nickname on Facebook, "handle" on Reddit and Yelp, and a fictitious character name on Twitter. He wondered why no one in his network found his profiles. Using the same name, even if it's a nickname, is important for brand continuity. If you use a nickname or abbreviation, write it as Charles "Chip" Smith, to let your personal and professional contacts know you wish to be addressed as "Chip" but they can find you online as "Charles."

5  **Routinely audit and purge your online connections.** Most of us who've been active on social media for many years have accumulated a large set of online connections. Periodically, go through your list of contacts and edit out anyone who (1) no longer serves your network, (2) has done something or posts about things you find distasteful, offensive or inappropriate, or (3) has hurt you. Often, it's easier to find people who fit categories 2 and 3, but not 1. Who are the people in your network who don't serve your career, brand or goals anymore? Consider people who may have been relevant to you in a previous career or time in your life, who may have been casual contacts then, but are too remote to invest time in cultivating today. Consider disconnecting from individuals who've changed their career or focus to an area that doesn't interest you or serve your needs. And, purge contacts who may have passed away. This last one is less often considered, but it's uncomfortable to send a mass message to your online contacts about an upcoming event with the title "Hope to see you there!" only to have someone's widow or widower remind you that you attended their funeral.

6  **Ensure your profiles are consistent and updated.** Do you use the same, or very similar, profile photos and language on all platforms? While LinkedIn is more professional in tone and Facebook is more casual, your profile information should speak to the same values, goals, skills and vision for your career. Strive for consistency across

all social media, so the visitor to your Instagram account who wants to learn more about you and checks your posts on Twitter sees the same person.

7 **If using brand colors or imagery, make them consisten across sites and platforms.** Some professionals today enjoy havig a custom logo for their personal brand. Others use a specific cor palette to reinforce their online presence. Across your websit blog, social media profiles and any avatars you might create se the same colors, look, tone and imagery to build consistencyf brand.

## With your presence

Maintaining reputational consistency in your look often the hardest for those of us who like to show different sides our personality in how we appear. Personally, I enjoy changing rstyles, wearing different outfits and changing up the way I presenyself to others. But, for brand consistency, I've learned to find ok that is appropriate for my audience and the situation, and ie with my values and the image I want to project. Projecting toany looks, within the same context, might confuse my audienceout the brand I'm representing.

Appropriateness is critical to managing tational risk. Ask yourself: What is appropriate for the messavant to convey and the audience I expect to receive it? When I nvited to deliver my TEDx Talk, the event organizers suggested senters come dressed casually. They had created a stage and set eatured local artists, with graffiti walls as the backdrop to our tnowing that I would be presenting about my work with the y, and my respect for our military is paramount, I pushed badressing casually. "My target audience for this message expesee me present myself consistent with a level of decorum and . I'll be dressed in business attire," I said. Looking back, I'm d I delivered a talk that has been viewed by tens of thousandsrans, active duty service members, military spouses and militporters and that I stayed "on brand" in my look (I wore a bri dress—my logo color— underneath a conservative blazer).

As you build out your wardrobe and presence to manage risk and stay on brand, consider:

1. **Does your look need updating?** If your brand could suffer because your presence reflects an outdated look, consider updating it. As we matte, some professionals update their looks to be more consistent with their elevated status or stature. While there are international trends to buck this belief (e.g., women don't have to wear their hair short when they hit "that certain age" and men can grow their beards long if they choose), you'll evaluate these options through the filter and lens of your brand and what feels most authentic to you. Also ask yourself if your current look reflects the values and goals you have today. In the past, it might have been acceptable, for instance, wear low-cut blouses (revealing cleavage), but today you serve a more conservative audience. They would likely want to see you dressed more professionally. Similarly, if you're used wearing shorts and sandals to work, as a client I worked with, but now you're meeting with conservative investors and bankers, you might need to include more appropriate items in your wardrobe. Your look should be consistent with your brand today. Consider updating your look (hairstyle and wardrobe) if it's been a while since you paid attention to it.

2. **Has your body changed?** Let's face it, over time gravity isn't always kind to bodies. If you've gained weight, lost weight or shifted how you carry your weight, it might be time to update your wardrobe. I've worked with clients (e.g., athletes) whose weight fluctuates depending on whether they're in training season or not. They might have sets of clothes for each season to accommodate their changing body. If the fit of your clothing is off-putting because it hangs loosely on your frame, or if it's too tight and seems to want to come off of you, your target audience might get distracted. Before it becomes an issue, take steps to update your look to be fitting for new body shape.

3. **Are you working remotely?** When stay-at-home orders were put in place around the world in 2020, many professionals found themselves ditching pantyhose and high heels for yoga pants

and slippers. When your work changes, you'll still need to be mindful of how you're appearing to others: even if that is on video instead of in person. Pay attention to the image you're projecting and whether it continues to maintain your brand and presence, even if you're working from home instead of an office.

4 **Are you feeding a negative narrative?** A successful attorney I knew often litigated cases in the courtroom. She was voluptuous and curvy and loved to play up her physical assets to get attention. Her clients didn't mind, nor did the other attorneys, but she had received negative input from the judges she presented to. In addition, there had been bloggers and legal journalists who pointed out her distracting presence and questioned whether she dressed this way to intentionally distract from a lack of skill or credibility. In her case, she had the option to dress as she wanted to and might have continued to attract questioning and ridicule. Instead, she opted to find a wardrobe that was still stylish and formfitting, but more appropriate to a courtroom setting where she litigated important cases. In another example, a male colleague of mine often wore a tussled hairstyle and partially grown beard (five o'clock shadow) that made him appear unkempt and sloppy. He embraced this look as rebellion for all the years he'd had to comb his hair into a look his parents deemed acceptable. His rebellion, however, undercut his credibility and he was often asked by prospective clients, "Did you just get out of bed?" or "Can you take our work seriously if you look like that?" and he'd even lost a key account because the client felt they couldn't let him speak to their board about an initiative they were presenting.

## Continually assess and refine your goals

As mentioned before, personal branding is not a linear, one-time event. Unfolding who you are and how you want to be known is a fluid, ongoing practice of assessment, refinement and results. As you're building your personal brand and reputation, continually evaluate your goals and progress to:

1  **Continue doing work that is meaningful and fulfilling.** You've worked hard to build this personal brand and earn the reputation you have today. Ensure your brand continues to bring you joy and rewards spiritually, financially, physically and emotionally. If your brand is only meeting one or two of those goals, perhaps some reconfiguring of your strategy is required. Or, if the marketplace shifts and the opportunities for everyone change, you might want to implement some short-term goals to adjust temporarily, ensuring you can return to your strategy when things are corrected.

2  **Reinforce expectations and timelines.** When you set your brand goals, were you realistic or did you set them too high or too low? Often times, setting goals at unrealistic levels or hedging them too much leads to poor choices. A goal that is too big of a stretch (such as "making partner in the firm by the end of my second year") without the necessary steps in place (Have you been at the firm long enough? Is your credibility intact? Do you have the endorsement and approvals of senior partners? Is the firm currently advancing people to partner level?) sets you up for disappointment. Not meeting this goal, then, could lead you to decide to change firms where you might face the same challenges. Similarly, setting your goals too low can give you a false sense of achievement. For example, if you strive to meet three new professional networking contacts this year, that should be easily attained quickly. You might then rest on your laurels and resist continuing to build your network because you believe you've met that goal. This would be unfortunate, as growing your professional network should be an ongoing process.

3  **If necessary, make changes to move closer to your goals and desired brand.** Consider that if your reputation growth and progress are showing only incremental advancement, do you need to shift bigger aspects of your life, such as doing different work or creating new relationships? There have been many times in my career when I've had to "level up" my visibility, skills, network and outreach to get to the next level of growth. While these times might be uncomfortable, they can be monumental. At times when I've felt

these growth plates shifting, and new opportunities are presenting themselves, I remind myself that as long as they are consistent with the brand I'm building, I'll stay open to them. When they have not been good for me, and represent risks to my commitment to my values, I've been able to confidently reject them.

4 **Remind yourself of your personal brand agreement** and commitment to seeing this process through. Remember, you will be tested for your conviction to stay the course of what you know is right for you. Resist the urge to grab the quick fix or the quick success and instead opt for what is crucial to maintain good brand health. Your goals, along with your values, will help you evaluate opportunities and ensure you'll make solid, low-risk choices.

## In closing

While discovering and building your personal brand can be invigorating and exciting, it is a process that requires attention and management to be successful and sustainable. Many clients have shared with me that when implementing their brand strategy, they were tempted to fall back into bad habits or patterns because mitigating risk and managing their reputation took effort. However, over time, living your brand and enjoying the rewards becomes commonplace— as you are being the version of yourself you designed!

Building something as important as your personal brand and reputation requires the same attention you would give any crucial career asset. You worked hard in school, you pushed forward in your career, you serve your clients and community with care. Similarly, you'll need to manage and nurture your brand. As much as reputation risk management is about what not to do (avoiding mistakes and risks), it is about pursuing the opportunities which a personal brand strategy will afford you. You will undoubtedly find yourself attracting more relationships, opportunities and places to share your gifts and talents, and being able to sift through those requires attention. From accepting LinkedIn connection invitations to partnering with colleagues on high-profile projects to modifying the way you present yourself to your clients, managing your brand is as important to the ongoing process of personal branding as the design and development phase.

## Endnote

**1** https://www.ftc.gov/enforcement/cases-proceedings/refunds/equifax-data-breach-settlement (archived at https://perma.cc/MM7W-P6E2)

# Final thoughts

*As we summarize the theories and application of personal branding highlighted in the book, we offer a final set of thoughts for you to consider as you set out to build your brand.*

When Aaron hired me, many years ago, he claimed he had an organizational problem at his company. "People don't know why they work here," he told me. "I need them to anchor into the brand of the company and see why we matter. I'm worried that key managers will leave because they don't seem happy." While organizational development work wasn't my specialty, Aaron was a family friend who believed I could help; I was intrigued by the scenario and agreed to get to work. One of the first steps I took was to observe where things weren't working. I set up shop in his office, observing the interactions among the team and interviewing team leaders on their understanding of the company's brand and value proposition. During many of the conversations about the company's future, the discussion turned to Aaron, the founder and CEO. His team described him as holding the company vision, being responsible for setting the mood of the teams (particularly the sales team) and steering the success of all employees. This was particularly interesting to me, as Aaron had said he wanted his employees to attach more to the company brand, not his.

One day, I asked to sit in on a sales team meeting and quickly identified a problem. During the meeting, Aaron sat at the head of the oval conference table. His sales staff flanked him on both sides and positioned their chairs towards him. There was very little banter or small talk as the meeting started. Aaron asked for an update on key accounts to which each account manager replied with short, succinct, factual replies. After each person spoke, all eyes quickly darted back to Aaron for a response, recommendation or reaction. A couple of times during the meeting, Aaron asked a question of the team, such as "Anyone seeing anything new from our competitors that we should be aware of?" or "What are clients saying about the new pricing?" to which no one responded. Instead, they'd all look at him for answers.

Everyone in the room knew of Aaron's extraordinary experience in the industry and his reputation as a "rainmaker" made him an admired boss. His team rarely spoke up in meetings, knowing his answer would inevitably be more insightful, revealing and impactful than their own. The room typically stayed silent for a few moments after he'd ask a question, and Aaron then answered his own questions to the applause of his team. Aaron seemed to delight in the accomplishment of having the right answer (yet again), and the group was dismissed. Afterwards, we discussed how he wanted his team to perceive him. I asked, what was his desired reputation? He told me it was important that they see him as being smart and knowledgeable, paving the way to success for them and relying on him for guidance. The more we talked, however, Aaron started to see that his own bias to being "large and in charge" and always being seen as the smartest person in the room was holding his team back. They weren't growing, learning and feeling empowered, and their careers at the company were at risk. The challenge, it turned out, wasn't that they weren't sold on the mission of the company. The problem was that Aaron was holding them back.

We discussed various behavior modification and style options and at the next meeting, Aaron mixed things up. As each account manager gave an account update, he pushed for more information, asking open-ended questions so the manager would be encouraged to expand on their initial update. Then, when he asked the group questions and they all waited for him to answer, he called out to individuals to give their insight or thoughts on the question. There are no wrong answers, he told the group, and they responded with some interesting and creative ideas. After the meeting, people seemed to smile more. They came to subsequent meetings a bit more hopeful. One account manager suggested a team retreat where they could brainstorm and strategize about growing key accounts, and Aaron recommended that individual lead the retreat, to their surprise and enjoyment! A few months later, I checked in with Aaron and he gave me an update:

> I'd always thought growing a company and a brand was about keeping things tightly controlled. I thought I had to prove myself to the team leaders, so they'd want to stay and learn from me. Now, I realize I was holding them back. By empowering and recognizing them individually, I grew the team value exponentially. They now bring ideas to me, seem happier at work, and are growing their accounts. It turns out that my personal brand had a lot to do with growing my company.

## Personal branding is just that: Personal

There may be nothing more personal, and nowhere we feel more vulnerable, than reputation. One client shared with me, "I'd be more inclined to show you my underwear drawer than look at how I'm perceived by others!" Opening ourselves up to examining our weaknesses and vulnerabilities, evaluating our values and goals, and believing we can take ownership of how we show up to others brings up feelings of being exposed, judged and critiqued. Most of us wouldn't volunteer for such scrutiny and evaluation unless we saw a direct and significant benefit. In the case of reputation management, the benefit is intention, control, and a sense of purpose and alignment unlike anything we receive elsewhere.

As we've discussed throughout this book, growing your reputation starts with setting the course of the brand you seek to build. How do you want to be perceived by the audiences that matter? The nature of the process (and the outcome) is inherently personal. You've undoubtedly experienced a whirlwind of emotions, thoughts, ideas and conflicts as you've navigated the pages of this book. Perhaps you jumped around in your reading as certain topics hit too close to home, returning to them later when you've had a moment to reflect. Maybe you've read through the book quickly, distancing yourself from the directness of the topics, only to realize later that you had work to do in unpacking your values and beliefs and creating a path forward that feels more intentional. And, perhaps some of the case studies and examples in this book brought to light areas where you can grow and develop as a leader, as a boss, as a parent or friend. Personal branding is a profoundly personal experience that involves many other people and results in a life and career well lived. Only then can you manage a reputation that is authentic, sustainable and scalable.

You may have also recognized that there are people in your network or circle who could benefit from learning how to bring forward their personal brand and direct their own reputation management. You might feel inclined to want to help them on the journey of self-reflection, discovery, design and deployment of their reputation journey. You now have the tools and insight to start that conversation and show them what you've learned. One bit of caution, however: Remember that their journey is their own. They have to be ready to hear the message, poised to take action on the recommendations and brave enough to look at the risks and challenges they might encounter. If they are, help them. If not, give them time. I'm often asked how I find new clients. What types of marketing do I send to people who should be focusing on their brands and reputation strategies? Actually, I do very little "marketing" of my work and services. I find it more helpful to speak and write on the topics covered here, to bring attention to the power and control you get through reputation management, and highlight the personal and professional joy you experience by using the processes and tools I've covered here. Then, when someone is inclined or ready, they find me. Or, they find another practitioner. Or, they try it themselves. The point is that I don't approach someone with a message of "You need personal branding!" in a hard sell. It's a personal journey that someone has to be ready to receive in order for the methodology and process to work.

## Reputations are fragile

I've seen that it can take years to develop and establish a reputation and a few swift actions to destroy one. Today, reputations are more fragile than ever because of internal and external forces. For example, the information superhighway, as it's called, brought us wonderful tools like social media, online services, streaming entertainment and telecommunications infrastructure that made it possible to collaborate, connect and learn from people around the world. It also brought us the potential for mistakes on a massive and global level. One offensive tweet, moral infraction or lapse of judgment can become a viral video or mob lightning rod, bringing everything you've ever done before into question and under scrutiny.

In my work over the years on reputation repair, I've assisted doctors and professors who crossed ethical lines and had intimate relationships with adult patients and students, which while consensual were inappropriate or in violation of their contracts; business leaders who thought to share or post an off-color video online that ended up getting them fired; professionals who inadvertently shared confidential information or intellectual property with competitors, putting the company and its future in jeopardy; and entrepreneurs who naively partnered with questionable investors and found their ethics and companies questioned at the highest levels. I've also seen firsthand how someone can do nothing wrong and suddenly find themselves in the midst of a reputation crisis because they were in the wrong place (or company) at the wrong time. I've seen teachers, professionals, consultants, coaches, business leaders and medical professionals who believed they were doing the right thing by staying silent about their circumstances and ended up being a scapegoat or not being protected by the institution or organization they thought would stand up for them. Rebuilding reputations is not easy or painless, regardless of whether you did something to create the situation or not.

The sections in this book on reputation monitoring and measurement, as well as the chapter on reputation risk management, should be referred to often. You will undoubtedly do much work to establish, pivot or repair your personal brand and reputation, and the process doesn't end there. Continually assess and rework the parts of the strategy that need to be modified to ensure you achieve the results you desire. It will feel easier over time, but there's never a time you'll not be mindful of how your behavior, relationships and narrative are supporting who you want to be positioned as, the legacy you desire and how you want your target audience to feel about you. One client described the maintenance process this way: "Just because I install new turf on my front lawn doesn't mean I'm done. I need to constantly tend to it, mow and fertilize it to make it grow." The analogy is clever and true. Over time, managing your reputation will become second nature and you'll make decisions that align with your goals without too much thought. But even then, regular watering and nurturing will ensure it continues to grow and thrive.

## Now you have the tools

You now have the tools and insight to move forward in your career with more intention and clarity. You've assessed where you're starting from and where you're headed. You've taken the bold step of identifying your ideal state—your desired reputation—and what it will take to get you there. You've considered the needs and wants of your target audience and aligned your value proposition in ways that will make you memorable, relevant and compelling to them. You've done the hard work. The branding part will certainly set you up to capitalize on opportunities as they arise and mitigate risks that may surface. Congratulations!

Living your brand will require patience, attention and thoughtfulness. At times, you may find yourself tempted away from the foundation that you've built. If this happens, rely upon your brand agreement to anchor back into those values and goals you've clearly said matter to you in building your legacy. If you make a mistake, quickly assess the impact (and any damage) and get back on the correct path to live congruously with how you aspire to be. Should you become the victim of a reputation attack or gaslighting, resist the urge to blame yourself and instead take advantage of the tools you have to regain your confidence and reputation, as you deserve.

The tools and guides presented in this book are not intended to be used individually. They work together to weave a tapestry of a reputation that can withstand outside pressures and negative influences, that is strong under scrutiny and is sustainable over time. To focus solely on your digital presence or networking and expect to receive the full benefits is not sufficient. The tools work together, building on each other and creating a complete view of who you are, what you value and what you offer. When someone views your social media, hears you introduce yourself, is referred to you by others or watches you in person, they expect to see the same person. While you can reveal different aspects of your personality and life to different audiences and in different situations, personal branding is about the consistency of the experience of working with you. If something seems off, out of sorts or "off brand," your audiences may grow concerned, confused or skeptical and leave you.

## What's coming in the future

Technology afforded us many advantages: Today, we can video chat with colleagues on the opposite side of the planet, our cars are learning to drive themselves, robots can deliver our medicine to us in the hospital and news travels as fast as the "return" key on a keyboard can strike. With all that technology provides, it hasn't replaced human interaction, empathy or our desire to be connected to others who offer us value, experience and relationship. As humans, we are logic- and emotion-driven beings that seek to trust, support and learn from the people we're attracted to. That's why personal branding will never go away and why reputation is so critical.

As you navigate the next chapters of your career, remember:

- **Stay fluid and flexible.** With each transition you'll endure in your career, embrace the opportunity to reassess, rediscover and realign your brand with your goals. In the future, this will become more important as geographic lines continue to blur for employees and leaders. It is possible that to lead in a company or community may require new nuances of reputation management we haven't seen yet. Cross-cultural teams and work styles may blend into one new norm for businesses and their leadership. Staying open to these changes, while grounded in your values and desired legacy, will keep you flexible enough to navigate these new paradigms.

- **Be mindful of the optics of your reputation.** No one besides you can know your true intentions, but others may judge you for what they witness. As more and more work is being done virtually, pay attention to how your communication, behavior and presence can create confusion with your target audiences. Seek alignment between who you are, what you value and what they need to know and feel. Even the appearance of inconsistency or impropriety can lead them to turn away.

- **Focus on your target audience.** They will endorse, support, encourage and refer you, and will continue to rely on your reputation to forgive any missteps. Colleagues will still refer to past experiences to understand uncharacteristic behavior. Investors will still refer to track record to predict future behavior. Reputation and brand will remain key ingredients to set the expectation of the experience others will have for working and being with you. Above all else, protect your reputation. You can rebuild a company. You can find new investors. You can rebuild your board of directors or your staff. But it is very hard to rebuild reputation. It is possible, as we've discussed here. But it's easier to not lose it in the first place.

- **Seek to understand.** You don't have to agree with others, but seek to listen, learn and embrace diversity of opinion and thought. Some of my greatest growth opportunities came when I trusted the process, my brand values and myself enough to listen before standing too firm in a belief. No one can make you feel something you don't want to, so the threat you might perceive may not be real. When you keep an open-minded view, you're more likely to appreciate another point of view or method, thus growing your own thinking and perspective.

- **Clarify who you are and why you do what you do.** Job titles change. Work changes. But who you are and why you're here is where your reputation grows in value. Resist the temptation to lock your personal sense of self to your professional title, degree or rank. Pedigree, work and status can often become confused with personal brand, and when that happens and a change ensues, separating the two can be painful. As more and more people become high profile in their industries and communities, the risk of closely tying the "what" to the "who" grows. I've been fortunate to help professional athletes, business leaders and technology pioneers navigate the complex process of separating what they do from who they are. The process requires a tremendous amount of courage and self-actualization, and the result is actually quite freeing and empowering.

- **Build community around you.** Without human interaction, we feel isolated and alone. Without credibility, we can't trust. Without reputation, we struggle to have an experience worth sharing. As information, business, social causes and ideas flow much more freely and rapidly today, the reputation someone brings into their leadership style, business growth, career, contribution and future is tantamount to success. We take a chance on someone who makes us feel they're worth hiring. We trust the doctor whose patients refer us to them. We visit the restaurant whose online reviews are glowing. Reputation is everything, and it's important to surround yourself with people who will support, encourage, endorse and refer you for the values you represent.

## Learn to stay in the question

A client once told me, "Sometimes you have to stay in the question a bit longer to find the answer." At the time, I was a young entrepreneur desperate to get things moving quickly and establish myself in my field. Patience was not my strongest virtue. His advice, however, was spot on. In our quest to find answers, solve problems, move forward and get results, we often miss the important things. We miss the tone in which feedback is offered, the sage wisdom in someone older's advice, the truth that a job loss is actually a blessing. In our rush to produce, finish, move to the next, rinse and repeat, we miss the gifts that are intended for us all along. What if all of those opportunities you missed were actually perfectly designed to get you where you are now, here, today? Reading through this book, I'm sure you still have questions. I'm sure there are parts that might not be crystal clear, given your situation or circumstances. Maybe you're fearful or uncertain about whether you deserve to be in control of your reputation or whether you truly could be perceived as valuable to the people who matter to you. Perhaps you're not sure on the timing to start the process or whether you have enough time left to build the legacy you desire.

With each question that arises, fight the urge to just answer it and move on. Reflect on the question. Consider different options and ideas. Consult close friends and colleagues. Ruminate on how you feel about the question and the answers that are coming forward for you. Run the question through your head (what do you think about it?), your gut (do the options sit right with you?) and your heart (how do I feel about my options?). Only when you are confident and clear about the answer should you move forward. Then, you'll know it was the right decision for you. Even if the outcome isn't immediately ideal, it was the direction you were supposed to take. What's right for you is right for you for reasons that only you can know. This is where the power of reputation management becomes truthful, authentic and purpose-driven, and where you truly can control the narrative of your life and legacy.

Your personal brand is the most intentional, authentic and compelling representation of your life, your values and your passions. When you can capture who you are, what you stand for and what you can offer in a reputation that is influential, inspiring and impactful, you will realize the power of controlling the narrative of your life and career.

# INDEX

CPSIA information can be obtained
at www.ICGtesting.com
Printed in the USA
JSHW011153250421
13941JS00001B/4

9 781398 600836